GW01157932

best | designed

Martin Nicholas Kunz . Patricia Massó

beach hotels

avedition

Locations

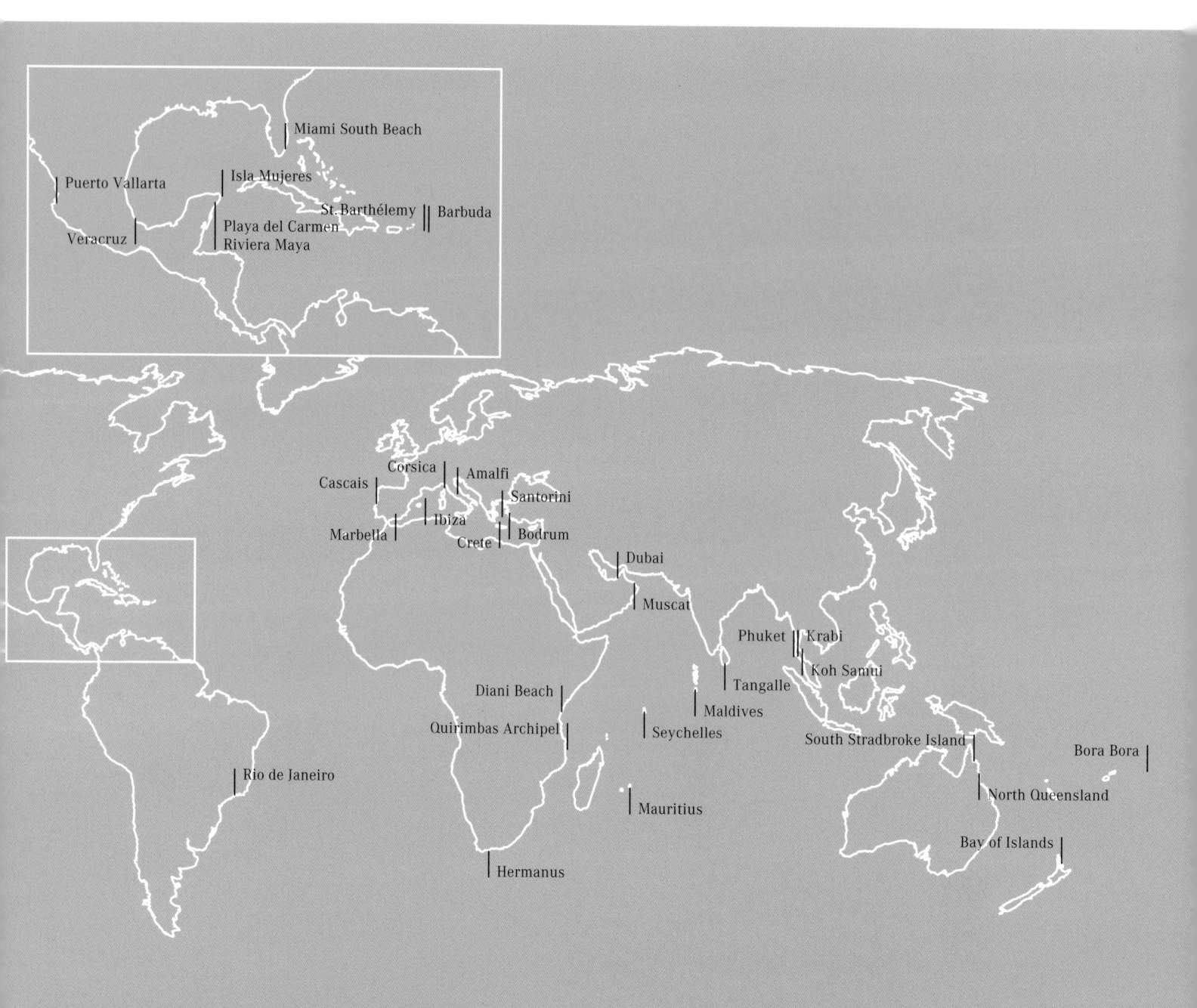

- Puerto Vallarta
- Veracruz
- Miami South Beach
- Isla Mujeres
- Playa del Carmen
- Riviera Maya
- St. Barthélemy
- Barbuda
- Cascais
- Corsica
- Amalfi
- Santorini
- Marbella
- Ibiza
- Crete
- Bodrum
- Dubai
- Muscat
- Phuket
- Krabi
- Koh Samui
- Diani Beach
- Tangalle
- Quirimbas Archipel
- Maldives
- Seychelles
- South Stradbroke Island
- Bora Bora
- Rio de Janeiro
- Mauritius
- North Queensland
- Bay of Islands
- Hermanus

EDITORIAL			4
Italy	Amalfi	Casa Angelina	8
France	Corsica	Casa del Mar	14
Spain	Ibiza	Ses Pitreras	18
	Marbella	The Beach House	22
Portugal	Cascais	Farol Design Hotel	26
Greece	Santorini	Ikies Traditional Houses	30
	Crete	Blue Palace Resort & Spa	34
Turkey	Antalya	Hillside Su	38
United Arab Emirates	Dubai	Madinat Jumeirah, the Arabian Resort	42
Oman	Muscat	The Chedi Muscat	46
Mauritius	Poste de Flacq	Constance Belle Mare Plage	52
	Wolmar	Taj Exotica Resort & Spa	56
Seychelles	North Island	North Island	60
Kenya	Diani Beach	Alfajiri Villas	64
Mozambique	Quirimbas Archipel	Matemo Island Resort	68
South Africa	Hermanus	Birkenhead House	72
Sri Lanka	Tangalle	Amanwella	78
	Bentota	Saman Villas	82
Maldives	North Male Atoll	Baros Maldives	86
	South Male Atoll	Anantara Resort Maldives	90
Thailand	Phuket	Aleenta Resort and Spa Phuket – Phangnga	94
	Krabi	Costa Lanta	100
	Koh Samui	Sala Samui Resort & Spa	104
Australia	Tropical North Queensland	Voyages Dunk Island	108
	South Stradbroke Island	Couran Cove Island Resort	112
New Zealand	Bay of Islands	Eagles Nest Kohanga Ekara	116
French Polynesia	Bora Bora	Bora Bora Nui Resort & Spa	120
Florida	Miami South Beach	The Setai	124
British West Indies	Barbuda	The Beach House Barbuda	128
Caribbean	St. Barthélemy	Eden Rock	132
Mexico	Puerto Vallarta	Las Alamandas	138
	Veracruz	Hotel Azúcar	142
	Riviera Maya	Esencia	146
	Isla Mujeres	Casa de los Sueños Resort and Spa	152
Brazil	Rio de Janeiro	Marina All Suites	156
HOTEL INDEX			160
ARCHITECTS & DESIGNERS / PHOTO CREDITS			167
IMPRINT			168

editorial | sun, sea, sand... design

A chilled Campari and soda on the hotel terrace just before sunset, with views of sailing boats and offshore islands. Breakfast under parasols and extra fluffy bathing towels. Lazy days that become blurred in the glimmering aqua marine blue of the ocean. Why is it, that just from the mere thought of a hotel by the beach, such a comforting feeling of relaxation washes over the body? There must be very few occasions which trigger off such similar euphoria-inducing expectations right away in the majority of people as the anticipation of a few easy-going days of vacation by the sea. Cliché or not: the prospect of aimlessly dozing away the time by an infinity pool that dissolves on the horizon, concentrating undisturbed on vacation reading under rustling palms and fragrant frangipani trees and later being able to bury your toes in the warm powder white sand comes pretty close to the vision of heaven on earth. Nothing against a cultured city trip, but even in an urban design hotel you are always on the go, trying not to miss out on any places of interest. A stylish beach retreat, on the other hand, suggests the quintessence of holiday and laissez-faire: not having to do anything and being allowed to do (almost) everything. Sheer relaxation and plenty of sun instead of sightseeing stresses and overambitious culture programs.

This "dolce vita" becomes the ultimate luxury, when the surroundings and the ambience are also right. When the swimming pool doesn't have that musty odor of chlorine and around it there are sufficient sun loungers available that aren't made of plastic, but of bamboo, rattan, teakwood or mahogany, covered with fresh towels every day. The perfectionism of this exquisite alfresco lounging comes from the Far East: the canopied, spacious day bed to protect from the tropical sun, which is no less than the rediscovery of the simple mattress, enticingly staged of course and a wonderful invitation for chilling The flowing transition between interior and exterior has also long since conquered the bathroom. Open-air showers have meanwhile become pretty much standard in a beach hotel, especially in tropical climates. There's no question about it, there's something both fun and stylish about swimming privatissimo in the ocean and then rinsing off the salt from your skin under the open sky. And sometimes a frog might even be watching you when you wake up in the morning. But the chances are pretty good that in such surroundings you'll already have your own prince nearby...

01 | Constance Belle Mare Plage

02 | Saman Villas

03 | Ikies Traditional Houses

04 | Baros Maldives

editorial | sand, sonne, meer... design

Zur blauen Stunde ein eisgekühlter Campari Soda auf der Hotelterrasse mit Blick auf Segelboote und vorgelagerte Inseln. Frühstück unter Sonnenschirmen und extra flauschigen Badehandtüchern. Faule Tage, die im flimmernden Aquamarinblau des Meeres verschwimmen. Wie kommt es bloß, dass sich allein schon beim Gedanken an ein Hotel am Strand so ein wohliges Gefühl von Entspannung im Körper breit macht? Es dürfte nur wenige Anlässe geben, die bei den meisten Menschen auf Anhieb eine ähnlich euphorisierende Erwartungshaltung auslösen wie die Vorfreude auf ein paar unbeschwerte Ferientage am Meer. Klischee hin oder her: Die Aussicht, an einem sich im Horizont auflösenden Infinity-Pool absichtslos dösend die Zeit zu vergessen, sich unter raschelnden Palmen und duftenden Frangipanibäumen ungestört auf die mitgebrachten Urlaubsschmöker zu konzentrieren und später seine Zehen in den warmen Puderzuckersand graben zu dürfen – diese Aussicht kommt der Vorstellung von einem irdischen Paradies schon ziemlich nahe. Nichts gegen einen kultivierten Städtetripp, doch selbst im urbanen Designhotel wird man immer ein wenig auf dem Sprung sein, um bloß keine Sehenswürdigkeit zu verpassen. Ein stilvolles Strandrefugium dagegen, das suggeriert die Quintessenz von Urlaub und Laisserfaire: Nichts tun zu müssen und (fast) alles tun zu dürfen. Erholung pur und Sonne satt anstelle von Besichtigungsstress und überambitionierten Kulturprogrammen. Zum absoluten Superluxus wird dieses Dolce Vita, wenn neben der Umgebung auch das Ambiente stimmt. Wenn es am Swimmingpool nicht nach Chlor muffelt und um das Becken genügend Liegestühle bereitstehen, die nicht aus Plastik, sondern aus Bambus, Rattan, Teakholz oder Mahagoni gefertigt sind und täglich mit frischen Badetüchern überzogen werden. Aus dem Fernen Osten stammt hierzu auch die Perfektionierung des exquisiten Abhängens im Freien: das zum Schutz vor der Tropensonne überdachte, ausladende Tagesbett, das nichts anderes ist als die Wiederentdeckung der einfachen Matratze, freilich verführerisch in Szene gesetzt und eine wunderbare Einladung zum Lümmeln. Der fließende Übergang zwischen drinnen und draußen hat längst auch die Badezimmer erobert. Open-Air-Duschen gehören inzwischen fast zum Standard eines Strandhotels, ganz besonders in tropischen Gefilden. Gar keine Frage, es macht nicht nur Spaß, sondern hat auch Stil, sich nach dem Schwimmen im Meer privatissimo und dennoch unter offenem Himmel das Salz von der Haut zu spülen. Und manchmal schaut einem morgens beim Wachwerden sogar ein Frosch zu. Als ob man in einer solchen Umgebung nicht schon längst einen Prinzen dabei hätte…

05 | Taj Exotica Resort & Spa

06 | North Island

07 | Matemo Island Resort

08 | Aleenta Resort and Spa Phuket – Phangnga

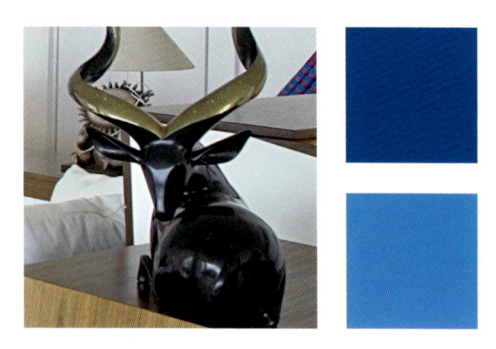

casa angelina | amalfi . italy

DESIGN: Marco de Luca, Francesco Savarese and Fusco Gennaro

Situated around 37 miles from Naples, the completely in white furnished building is enthroned on a steep coast on the Gulf of Salerno, between Amalfi and Positano. Its location in the cliffs and the fantastic views of the sea alone are what makes this hotel so appealing. These natural factors are amplified by the emphasized casual design, which is more reminiscent of Ibiza chill-out than a classic Southern Italian coastal hotel. With only 41 rooms and suites the hotel is a lifestyle boutique resort, and appeals to more of a younger clientele, who places great value on lots of privacy. On terraces, in the lounge, restaurant, corridors, halls and rooms is white upholstered furniture, long curtains that blow in the breeze or white four poster beds on dark wooden floors. The planners have consistently avoided the use of colors and have selected color-coordinated materials or materials with deliberately contrasting details. The rather minimal interior almost seems like a museum, where the unusual collection of contemporary objets d'art made of Murano glass is shown off to its best advantage. If you get cozy here and don't feel like sightseeing, you can just sit back, relax and enjoy the service. Nothing is lacking, neither a bar or good food in the restaurant, nor a beach, which is even accessible to hotel guests via the panoramic elevator.

Rund 60 Kilometer von Neapel entfernt, thront das ganz in Weiß gehaltene Gebäude auf einer Steilküste am Golf von Salerno, zwischen Amalfi und Positano. Alleine schon die Lage in den Klippen und die traumhafte Aussicht aufs Meer üben dabei ihren Reiz aus. Verstärkung erfahren diese naturgegebenen Faktoren noch von der betont lässigen Gestaltung, die eher an ein Ibiza-Chillout erinnert als an ein klassisches süditalienisches Küstenhotel. Mit nur 41 Zimmern und Suiten positioniert es die Betreibergesellschaft Steinhotels als Lifestyle-Boutique-Resort und spricht eher ein jüngeres Klientel an, das Wert auf viel Privatsphäre legt. Auf Terrassen, in Lounge, Restaurant, Fluren, Hallen und Zimmern weiß gepolstertes Mobiliar. Lange, sich im Wind wiegende Vorhänge oder weiße Himmelbetten auf dunklen Holzböden. Durchweg sind die Planer sparsam mit dem Einsatz von Farben umgegangen und haben Materialien Ton in Ton oder in Details bewusst kontrahierend ausgewählt. Das eher reduzierte Interieur schafft so auch den fast schon musealen Rahmen, um die ungewöhnliche Sammlung zeitgenössischer Kunstobjekte aus Murano-Glas zur Geltung zu bringen. Wer es sich hier einmal gemütlich gemacht hat und keine Lust auf Besichtigungsprogramme hat, kann sich hier auch entspannt zurücklehnen und den Service genießen. Es fehlt an nichts, weder an einer Bar noch an gutem Essen im Restaurant und schon gar nicht an einem Strand. Der ist sogar nur von den Gästen mit einem Panorama-Aufzug erreichbar.

01 | The outdoor pool invites you for a refreshing cool-down.
Zu einer erfrischenden Abkühlung lädt der Außenpool ein.

02

03

02 | The dominating color of white gives the resort its freshness.

Die dominierende Farbe Weiß gibt dem Resort seine Frische.

03 | A panoramic view over the Mediterranean can be admired from the hotel terrace.

Von der Hotelterrasse bietet sich ein Panoramablick auf das Mittelmeer.

04 | Bubbling wellbeing-experience: the indoor pool with attached spa area.

Sprudelndes Wohlfühl-Erlebnis: Das Hallenbad mit angeschlossenem Wellnessbereich.

05 | Club atmosphere in the lounge.

Clubatmosphäre in der Lounge.

06 | A collection of Murano glass objects gives the area a museum flair.

Eine Sammlung aus Murano-Glas-Objekten verleiht den Räumlichkeiten ein museales Flair.

05
06

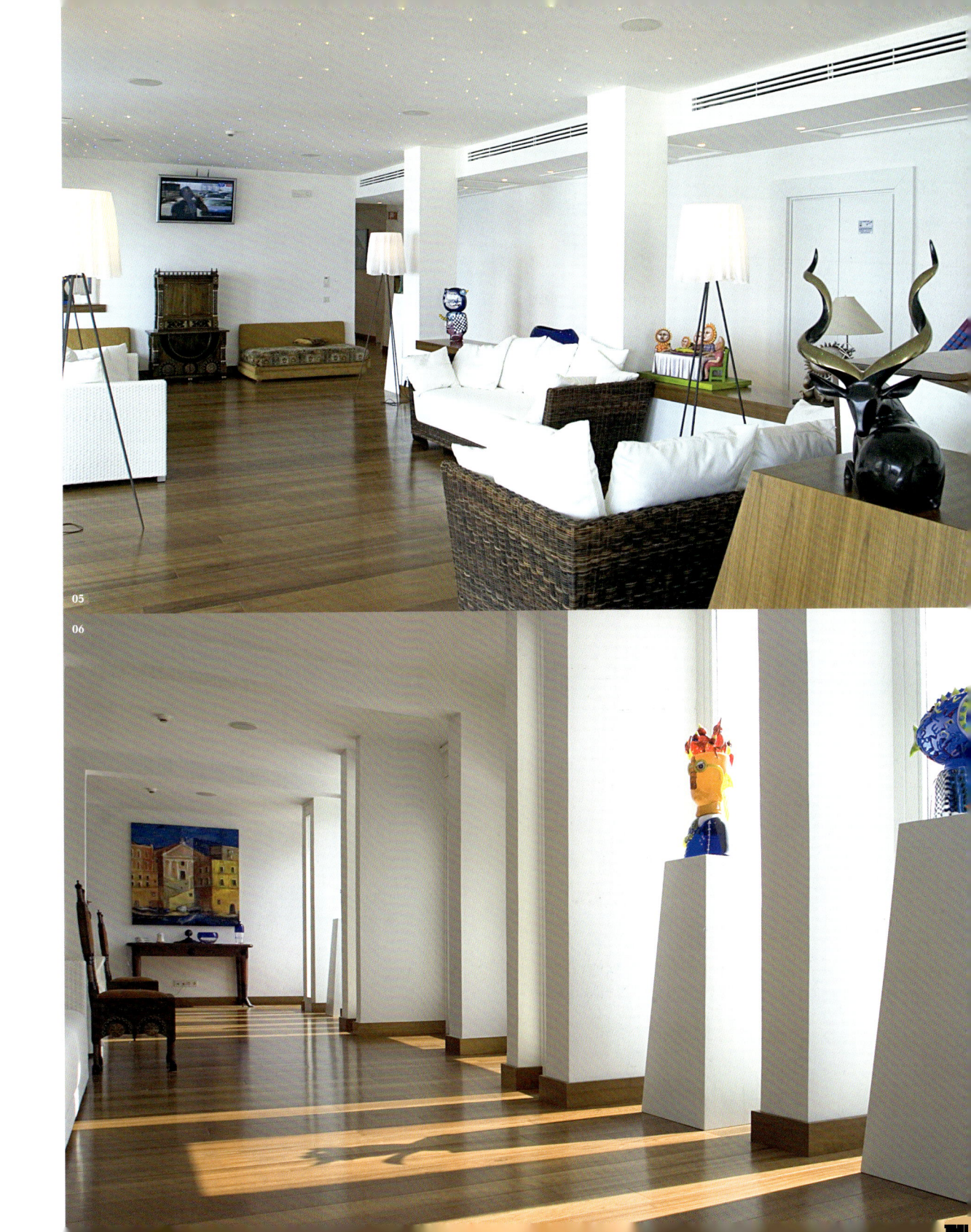

01 | Living in nature whilst shaping it–the meticulously planned entrance area is representative of the entire hotel.

In der Natur Leben und sie gestalten – der sorgfältig angelegte Eingangsbereich steht stellvertretend für das gesamte Hotel.

casa del mar | corsica . france
DESIGN: Jean Francois Bodin, Carole Marcellesi

The special lies in the ordinary. Based on this principle are the furnishings of the Mediterranean house, where the main focus is on the use of natural raw materials. Everything that the local environment has to offer has been used here and transformed into something unique. This doesn't just apply to the fresh ingredients, which come under the knife every day in the in-house restaurant, but also to the materials used in the interior design. The beds are made from natural woods, just as the specifically installed paneling and floorings. The colors of nature are reflected in the twelve suites and eight rooms. The glowing red of a field poppy, the brilliant blue of the sky and the intense lilac of lavender create very special effects on armchairs, rugs, fabrics and tables. Thereby every room has been assigned an expressive color, which combined with white and cream tones, is more lively than loud. Another extra special touch is provided by design classics, which are easily combined with the rest of the furnishings. Every room has its own terrace with views over the mountain-lined Porto-Vecchio bay. Guests can also enjoy this view from the private beach of the house. Of course they can also be active and explore the bay whilst water skiing, diving or in a canoe.

Das Besondere liegt im Einfachen. Auf diesem Grundsatz beruht die Einrichtung dieses mediterranen Hauses. Dabei liegt ein Schwerpunkt auf dem Einsatz natürlicher Rohstoffe. Alles, was die Umgebung zu bieten hat, hat man genutzt und in etwas Einzigartiges verwandelt. Das gilt nicht nur für die frischen Zutaten, die täglich im hauseigenen Restaurant unters Messer kommen, sondern auch für die Materialien der Inneneinrichtung. Die Betten sind aus naturbelassenen Hölzern, genau wie die gezielt eingesetzten Vertäfelungen und Bodenbeläge. Die Farben der Natur finden sich in den zwölf Suiten und acht Zimmern wieder. Das leuchtende Rot des Klatschmohns, das strahlende Blau des Himmels und das intensive Lila des Lavendels erzielen auf Sesseln, Teppichen, Stoffen und Tischen eine ganz besondere Wirkung. Dabei ist jedem Raum eine aussagekräftige Farbe zugeordnet, die mit Weiß und Cremetönen kombiniert, lebendig, aber nicht laut wirkt. Für eine weitere besondere Note sorgen Designklassiker, die locker mit dem übrigen Mobiliar kombiniert sind. Jedes Zimmer hat eine eigene Terrasse mit Blick auf die von Bergen gesäumte Porto-Vecchio Bucht. Ihren Anblick kann der Gast auch vom Privatstrand des Hauses genießen. Natürlich kann er auch selbst aktiv werden und die Bucht beim Wasserski, beim Tauchen oder mit dem Kanu erkunden.

02

02 | The red junior suite shows, how modern design harmonizes with natural materials.
Die rote Junior Suite zeigt, wie modernes Design mit natürlichen Materialien harmoniert.

03 | The heated pool is surrounded by a well-looked after, Mediterranean garden.
Der beheizte Pool ist vom gepflegten mediterranen Garten umgeben.

01 | The illuminated pool is also perfect for a nighttime dip.
Der beleuchtete Pool lädt auch nachts noch zum Bad ein.

ses pitreras | ibiza . spain
DESIGN: Joan Lao

The famous Ibiza feeling, this good mood blend of a careless zest for life, Mediterranean flair, hippy nonchalance and party spirit is in the air at Ses Pitreras. Tamed and cultivated in a newly-designed building from the 70's, with only seven guest rooms it radiates an almost family-like atmosphere. Architects have retained the Spanish architectural style with its whitewashed walls and shady wooden pergolas and complemented it with contemporary design and furniture. Every room is decorated differently. Fresh colors provide a young and trendy atmosphere, everything but cluttered. After dancing the night away, you can recover in solitude in the garden and by the swimming pool, under illuminated bougainvilleas and palm trees. The hotel is open all year round. And in the unlikely event that the sun should not shine for an extended period, a solarium is available to top-up your tan. The young service team serves fresh Mediterranean cuisine with a Basque influence. The hotel bar—as it should be on an island like Ibiza—is open around the clock. However if boredom starts to creep in, you can book a boat trip in Ses Pitreras to the small neighboring island of Formentera.

Das berühmte Ibiza-Feeling, diese Gute-Laune-Mischung aus unbekümmerter Lebensfreude, mediterranem Flair, Hippie-Lässigkeit und Partystimmung ist auch im Ses Pitreras spürbar. Gezähmt und kultiviert in einem neu gestalteten Gebäude aus den 70er-Jahren. Mit nur sieben Gästezimmern strahlt es eine fast familiäre Atmosphäre aus. Den spanischen Baustil mit seinen weiß gekalkten Mauern und schattenspendenden hölzernen Pergolas haben die Architekten beibehalten und durch zeitgemäßes Design und Mobiliar ergänzt. Jedes Zimmer ist anders eingerichtet, in frischen Farben, jung, trendig und alles andere als überladen. Nach einer durchtanzten Nacht kann man sich in aller Abgeschiedenheit im Garten und am Swimming-Pool, unter leuchtenden Bougainvilleas und Palmen erholen. Das Hotel ist rund ums Jahr geöffnet. Und falls die Sonne, was unwahrscheinlich ist, für längere Zeit einmal nicht scheinen sollte, steht ein Solarium für den Bräune-Ausgleich bereit. Das junge Serviceteam serviert frische Mittelmeerküche mit baskischem Einschlag. Die Hotelbar ist – wie es sich für eine Insel wie Ibiza gehört – rund um die Uhr geöffnet. Wem es dennoch langweilig werden sollte, der kann im Ses Pitreras einen Bootsausflug zur kleinen Schwesterinsel Formentera buchen.

02 | 03 Inside ground natural stone flooring and walls meet rough wooden ceilings.

In den Innenräumen treffen geschliffene Natursteinböden und Wände auf raue Holzdecken.

04 | 05 The pool with its wooden deck and the restaurant are the center of communication.

Der Pool mit seinem Holzdeck und das Restaurant sind kommunikativer Mittelpunkt.

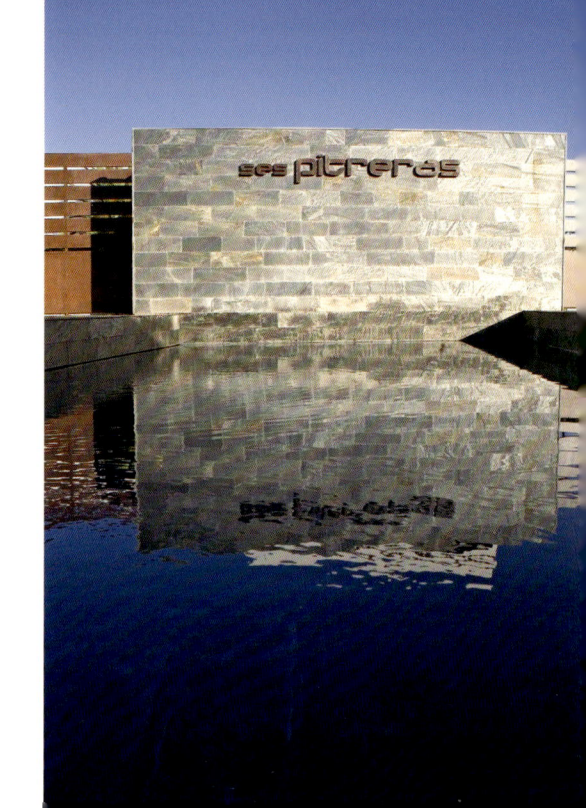

05

01 | Mediterranean elements have been combined with cool elegance.
Mediterrane Elemente wurden kombiniert mit cooler Eleganz.

the beach house | marbella . spain
DESIGN: Kjell Sporrong

The rich and the beautiful are at home in Marbella. If you don't have a permanent home in the resort of the international jet set, yet would still like to enjoy the benefits of a private luxury villa, you can rent out The Beach House. The private guest house is located right on the beach between Málaga and Marbella. The house only has ten exclusive guest rooms. This is what makes it such a distinctly individual abode. At the same time it is regarded as one of the hippest small hotels in Marbella. The designers have paid particular attention to stylish and exclusive design. Guests can also purchase and take home with them many of the decorative items, like porcelain, crystal or pictures. But the love for detail and especially for cool elegance is not only found again in the rooms and the bar lounge. Complementing the interior is the beach house chill-out music collection, mixed by the trendiest DJs of Marbella and the French Riviera. The entire house can be rented to guests for events, birthday parties or similar events. Numerous golf courses in the immediate surroundings and the Club Hípico El Dorado riding school offer a sporty alternative program to Marbella's exciting party scene. You can refuel your energy by the pool with sea view or at the open fireplace.

Die Schönen und Reichen sind in Marbella zu Hause. Wer am Ferienort des internationalen Jetsets keinen festen Wohnsitz hat und trotzdem die Vorzüge einer privaten Luxusvilla genießen möchte, der mietet sich in das The Beach House ein. Die private Pension liegt direkt am Strand zwischen Málaga und Marbella. Das Haus verfügt lediglich über zehn exklusive Gästezimmer. Dies macht es zu einem ausgesprochen individuellen Domizil. Gleichzeitig gilt es als eines der angesagtesten kleinen Hotels in Marbella. Die Macher haben besonders auf ein stilvolles und exklusives Design geachtet. Viele der Dekorationsstücke wie etwa Porzellan, Kristall oder Bilder werden auch zum Nachkauf und zum mit nach Hause nehmen angeboten. Die Liebe zum Detail und vor allem zur coolen Eleganz findet sich aber nicht nur in den Zimmern und der Bar Lounge wieder. Passend zum Interieur gibt es die beach house chill-out-music collection, komponiert von den trendigsten DJs Marbellas und der französischen Riviera. Für Kundenevents, Geburtstagsfeiern und Ähnliches kann gleich das gesamte Haus gemietet werden. Zahlreiche Golfplätze in der unmittelbaren Umgebung und die Reitschule Club Hípico El Dorado bieten ein sportliches Alternativprogramm zur aufregenden Partyszene Marbellas. Die notwendigen Kräfte tankt man am Pool mit Meerblick oder an der offenen Feuerstelle.

02 | The pool is heated all year round.
Der Pool ist das ganze Jahr beheizt.

03 | Privacy, just like in your own villa.
Privatsphäre, wie in der eigenen Villa.

04 | Not all of the ten rooms have a TV.
Nicht alle der zehn Zimmer haben TV.

05 | Great value is placed on persönlichen Service.
Großen Wert wird auf persönlichen Service gelegt.

03
04
05

01 | The balconies of the rooms gradually step down into the terraces and cliffs. There are sandy bays between the rocks all along the coast.

Stufenweise gehen die Balkone der Zimmer in die Terrassen und Klippen über. Zwischen den Felsen gibt es der Küste entlang auch immer wieder Sandbuchten.

farol design hotel | cascais . portugal

DESIGN: Cristina Santos Silva & Ana Meneses Cardoso, Carlos Miguel Dias (CM DIAS Arquitectos), Angela Basto & Paula Castro, Ana Salazar, José António Tenente, António Augustus, João Rôlo, Fátima Lopes, Miguel Vieira, Paulo Matos, Manuel Alves & José Manuel Gonçalves, Paulina Figueiredo, Arkadius

What first stands out is the location: The hotel building sits enthroned on rocks over the Atlantic surf and facing the water. On the grounds nearby is the old Santa Marta light house, which guided the first sailors of medieval times safely around the cliffs. The heart of the hotel lives in a villa from the year 1890, formerly owned by the Count of Cabral now it has been completely renovated and expanded given a new infrastructure by the new owners in 2002. This is where you'll find the lobby, restaurant and bar. Most of the 31 guest rooms and three suites, as well as the two conference rooms are in the new section. Its linear design features floor to ceiling glass windows, which bring lots of light into the rooms and visually incorporate the nature on the other side. The rooms, designed in different colors and materials, have parquet floors in the interiors and wooden terraces or balconies with light marble floors in the exteriors. The pool, bar and disco offer relaxation and entertainment right on the hotel's doorstep. Or you can pay a visit to the Casino Estoril, the biggest in Europe, which is only five minutes away. For the sportier guests there are ten golf courses nearby, as well as riding, tennis or sailing and other water sports.

Was zuerst auffällt, ist die Lage: Das Hotelgebäude thront auf Felsen über der Atlantikbrandung und ist zu 180 Grad von Wasser umgeben. Auf dem Gelände direkt daneben steht der alte Santa Marta Leuchtturm, der die ersten Seefahrer des Mittelalters sicher um die Klippen geleitet hat. Das Herz des Hotels schlägt in einer Villa aus dem Jahr 1890, die ehemals im Besitz des Grafen von Cabral war. Die neuen Besitzer haben sie 2002 komplett umgebaut, erweitert und mit einer neuen Infrastruktur versehen. Hier findet man die Lobby, das Restaurant und die Bar. Die meisten der 31 Gästezimmer und drei Suiten sowie die beiden Konferenzräume sind im neuen Trakt. Er präsentiert sich mit einer geradlinigen Bauweise mit raumhohen Verglasungen, was viel Licht in die Räume bringt und die Natur optisch mit einbezieht. Die in unterschiedlichen Farben und Materialien gestalteten Zimmer haben innen Parkettböden und außen Holzterrassen oder Balkone mit hellen Marmorböden. Entspannung und Unterhaltung direkt vor der Haustüre bieten Pool, Bar und Diskothek. Oder man besucht das nur fünf Minuten entfernte Casino Estoril, das größte in Europa. Für die Sportlichen gibt es zehn Golfplätze in der Umgebung sowie Reiten, Tennis oder Segeln und anderen Wassersport.

02 | 03 Ten different stylists left their individual trademarks in the design of the rooms. The selection is just as varied.

Zehn verschiedene Stylisten hinterließen ihre individuelle Handschrift bei der Raumgestaltung. Entsprechend vielfältig ist die Auswahl.

04 | The guest rooms can be found on the upper floor of the new building.

Im oberen Stockwerk des Neubaus befinden sich die Gästezimmer.

04

01 | Deep below the "Ikies" stretches the Aegean Sea.
Tief unter dem „Ikies" erstreckt sich die Ägäis.

ikies traditional houses | santorini . greece
DESIGN: Akis Charalambous

In the azure blue water of the Greek Aegean, some hundred miles away from Crete, is the island of Santorini. The island is dominated by an extinct volcano and the ridgeline is fringed with snow white little houses– the "Ikies" villa retreats. Three studios, three maisonette rooms and four suites are housed in the rambling building. The elegant abodes, with a minimal design, are thematically furnished and have names like "House of the Boatman", "House of the Antiquarian" or "House of the Winemaker". Cast-iron beds, terracotta floors and antique furniture emphasize the authentic ambience of the rooms, which were carved out of pumice. Guests can enjoy a drink at the bar after swimming in the pool. Or sit on your own terrace. Every room in the hotel has alfresco seating. From here you can look out over the sea or the mighty volcano crater. While the crater wall steeply slopes down the west side of the island, the gently curved east coast of Santorini invites you to sunbathe and swim in its long beaches. It's also not far to the Capital Thira with its winding side streets and vaulted steps.

Im azurblauen Wasser der griechischen Ägäis, etwa 100 Kilometer von Kreta entfernt, erstreckt sich die Insel Santorin. Das Eiland wird durch einen erloschenen Vulkan dominiert, dessen Kammlinie von schneeweißen Häuschen gesäumt ist – der Villenanlage Ikies Traditional Houses. Drei Studios, drei Maisonette-Zimmer und vier Suiten beherbergen die verwinkelten Gebäude. Die elegant-minimalistisch konzipierten Domizile sind thematisch eingerichtet und tragen Namen wie „Haus des Bootsmannes", „Haus des Antiquars" oder „Haus des Winzers". Gusseiserne Betten, Terrakottaböden und antikes Mobiliar unterstreichen dabei das authentische Ambiente der Zimmer, die aus Bimsstein gemauert wurden. Gäste, die im Pool schwimmen, genießen anschließend einen Drink an der Bar. Oder aber sie sitzen auf der eigenen Terrasse. Jedes Zimmer im Hotel verfügt über eine Sitzgelegenheit an der frischen Luft. Von hier aus blickt man aufs Meer oder den mächtigen Vulkankrater. Während die Kraterwand zur Westseite der Insel hin steil abfällt, lädt die sanft geschwungene Ostküste Santorins mit ihren langen Stränden zum Sonnen und Baden ein. Auch in der Hauptstadt Thira, mit seinen verwinkelten Gassen und übermauerten Treppengängen, ist es nicht weit.

02 | Accentuated by color: one of the spacious bathrooms.
Farblich akzentuiert: Eines der geräumigen Badezimmer.

03 | Cast iron beds are a part of the authentic furnishings.
Gusseiserne Betten sind Teil der authentischen Einrichtung.

04 | Guests can meet for a drink on the roomy terrace.
Auf der weitläufigen Terrasse treffen sich die Gäste auf einen Drink.

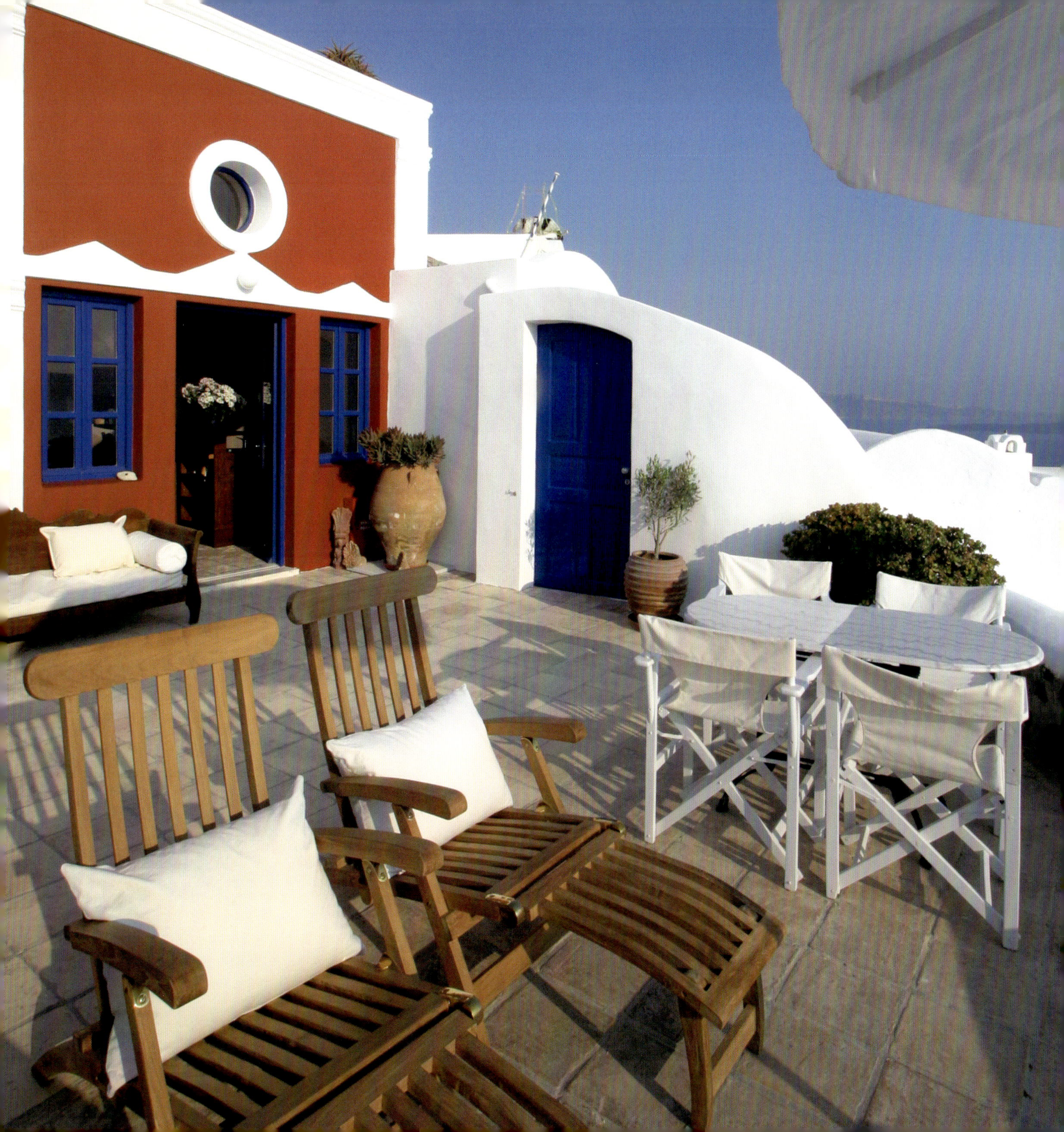

01 | Classicism is given a new twist by the turquoise colored pool.
Am türkisfarbenen Pool wird die Klassik neu interpretiert.

blue palace resort & spa | crete . greece

DESIGN: Team around Angelos Angelopoulos, 3SK Stylianides, Costantza Sbokou

By the swimming pool Greek classicism takes a post modern twist: with constructive boldness, neo-antique grandezza and the nonchalant sacrifice on functionality the terracotta-colored wall with its round arch is set in the turquoise blue water. This original, mismatched feature has style and gives the holiday resort the flair of a modern palace. The elegant Blue Palace Resort & Spa is situated on the north-east coast of Crete, two miles away from the village of Elounda. Despite having 254 rooms and suites, guests can find peace and solitude in the rooms, which are scattered between palm and olive trees and several individual bungalows, built into the cliffs. You can catch a glance of the glistening Cretian Sea from everywhere in this hotel and watch out for ships and sailing boats. Another eye turner is the offshore island of Spinalonga with its medieval fort. And if you favor swimming in the sea rather than the pool, hop into the panorama lift and be transported to the 656 foot-long hotel beach. And if you don't want to get back in the lift to go for lunch, just stay where you are and satisfy your hunger with freshly caught squid from the grill at the hotel's beach taverna. Recommended to care for sun-damaged skin is a Thalasso treatment in the Elounda Spa, which is also situated on the beach on over 21,500 square feet.

Am Swimmingpool schlägt die griechische Klassik eine postmoderne Kapriole: Mit konstruktiver Kühnheit, neo-antiker Grandezza und dem nonchalenten Verzicht auf Funktionalität lässt die terrakottafarbene Mauer ihren Rundbogen im türkisblauen Wasser wurzeln. Diese originelle, unangepasste Geste hat Stil und verleiht dem Ferienresort das Flair eines modernen Palastes. Das elegante Blue Palace Resort & Spa liegt an der Nordostküste von Kreta, drei Kilometer von der Ortschaft Elounda entfernt. Trotz der immerhin 254 Zimmer und Suiten finden die Gäste hier Ruhe und Abgeschiedenheit, denn die Räume verteilen sich zwischen Palmen und Olivenbäumen auf mehrere, in die Klippen eingebettete Einzelbungalows. Von überall kann der Blick über das glitzernde kretische Meer schweifen und nach Schiffen und Segelbooten Ausschau halten. Ein weiterer Blickfang ist die vorgelagerte Insel Spinalonga mit ihrer mittelalterlichen Festung. Wer das Baden im Meer dem Pool vorzieht, steigt in den Panoramaaufzug und lässt sich zum 200 Meter langen hoteleigenen Strand herunterbringen. Und wer auch zum Mittagessen nicht wieder in den Aufzug steigen möchte, bleibt einfach unten und stillt seinen Hunger in der hoteleigenen Strandtaverne mit fangfrischen Tintenfischen vom Grill. Zur Pflege der sonnenstrapazierten Haut empfiehlt sich eine Thalassobehandlung im Elounda Spa, dessen mehr als 2000 Quadratmeter ebenfalls am Strand liegen.

02

02 | Wooden flooring gives the bedroom a warm touch.
Der Holzfußboden gibt dem Schlafzimmer eine warme Note.

03 | The offshore island of Spinalonga can be seen from the veranda.
Von der Veranda aus ist die vorgelagerte Insel Spinalonga zu sehen.

04 | When the weather cools it's also possible to swim inside.
Bei kühlem Wetter kann man auch drinnen schwimmen.

01 | Relaxing or observing passers-by is no problem here. The giant mirror is made for "people watching."

Ausruhen oder Fleischbeschau, das ist hier „keine" Frage. Der riesige Spiegel parodiert „people watching".

hillside su | antalya . turkey

DESIGN: Eren Talu, Yael Bahior, Asli Eke, Merve Yoneyman

A shining concrete structure over seven-stories soars from the ground on the Turkish Riviera with its long beaches, orange groves and cliffs. The contrast is intentional. For ten long years the Hillside Leisure Group and Eren Talu worked meticulously on the concept. It provokes conventional expectations. Even in the lobby, where oversized disco balls hang down for over 66 feet from the ceiling. This interplay of white architecture with mirrors and light effects runs through the whole house, from the reception, to the gastronomy, through to the 294 apartments and 41 suites. Even if you like coziness you'll have to enjoy it in white here. Everything is white, even the televisions. But cushioned areas and seating alcoves made of white leather are perfected for relaxed chilling. Only light installations and lava lamps provide the color. To recharge your batteries after nights of partying, the hotel provides a palette of extras for recreation: mattresses under straw covered sun shades, heated indoor and outdoor swimming pools with underwater sound, substantial spa menus or tennis and squash.

Über sieben Stockwerke ragt ein blanker Betonkörper aus dem Boden, an der türkischen Riviera mit ihren langen Stränden, Orangenhainen und Klippen. Der Kontrast ist gewollt. Zehn Jahre lang tüftelte die Hillside Leisure Group um Eren Talu an dem Konzept. Es provoziert herkömmliche Erwartungen. Etwa die Lobby: Von der Decke hängen aus über 20 Metern übergroße Diskokugeln herunter. Dieses Zusammenspiel von weißer Architektur mit Spiegeln und Lichteffekten durchzieht das ganze Haus, vom Empfang, über die Gastronomie bis in die 294 Appartments und 41 Suiten. Wer es kuschelig mag, muss das in Weiß ausleben. Alles ist weiß, selbst der Fernseher. Polsterlandschaften und Sitznischen aus weißem Leder lassen einen aber lässig abhängen. Für Farbe sorgen nur Lichtinstallationen und Lavalampen. Um die Akkus nach den Partynächten wieder aufzutanken, hält das Hotel eine Palette von Extras zur Rekreation bereit: Matratzen unter strohbedeckten Sonnenschirmen, beheizte Innen- und Außen-Schwimmbäder mit Unterwassersound, reichhaltige Spa Menüs oder Tennis und Squash.

02 03

40 | hillside su

02 | The extravagant entrance fascinates with its modern architecture and lighting.
Der extravagante Eingang fasziniert mit moderner Architektur und Lichtreflexen.

03 | Lounge.
Lounge.

04 | Wooden deck on the sandy beach.
Holzdeck am Sandstrand.

madinat jumeirah, the arabian resort | dubai . united arab emirates
DESIGN: KCA International, Khuan Chew, Design Principal, Mirage Mille

Mighty wind towers, which previously were used to cool buildings, characterize the architecture of this hotel facility, an Arabian village style stretching two miles along the sea. Waterways meander through the resort with its colorful souk, a spice market and countless small shops. With the traditional water taxis, which also travel along the Creek estuary into the city center of Dubai, guests can reach the 45 different restaurants and bars or be chauffeured to one of the two hotels Mina A'Salam and Al Quasr or Dar Al Masyaf with its 28 Arabian Summer Houses. At nightfall hundreds of lights illuminate the façades, structured with arcs and windows, like a palace from 1001 Nights. Lattices made of geometrical braided patterns in the windows and arch openings emphasize the Oriental atmosphere, which can also be found in the rooms that are at least 538 square feet and feature dark richly carved wooden furniture. With this concept the Jumeirah Group wants to preserve the cultural heritage of the golf region and show what Arabian hospitality is all about. Another highlight is the Six Senses Spa, with its color scheme of subtle green and off-white. With its 28 free standing treatment studios, surrounded by gardens full of flowers and waterways, it's the biggest spa facility in the Middle East. One section completely screened off from the public—in accordance with Arabian tradition—is reserved exclusively for women.

Mächtige Windtürme, die früher für natürliche Kühlung sorgten, prägen die Architektur der Hotelanlage, die sich im Stil eines arabischen Dorfes auf einer Länge von 3,7 Kilometern am Meer entlangzieht. Wasserwege mäandern durch das Resort mit seinem farbenfrohen Souk, einem Gewürzmarkt und zahllosen kleinen Geschäften. Gäste können mit den traditionellen Wassertaxis, die auch den Creek, den Meeresarm im Stadtzentrum Dubais, befahren, die 45 verschiedenen Restaurants und Bars erreichen oder sich in eines der zwei Hotels Mina A'Salam und Al Quasr oder Dar Al Masyaf mit seinen 28 Arabian Summer Houses chauffieren lassen. Nachts lassen hunderte von Lichtern die mit Bögen und Fenstern gegliederte Fassade wie einen Palast aus Tausendundeiner Nacht erscheinen. Gitterwerke aus geometrischen Flechtmustern in den Fenstern und Bogenöffnungen unterstreichen das orientalische Ambiente, das sich auch in den mindestens 50 Quadratmeter großen Zimmern, mit ihren dunklen reich geschnitzten Holzmöbeln wieder findet. Die Jumeirah Gruppe will mit diesem Konzept das kulturelle Erbe der Golfregion bewahren und zeigen, was das Wesen arabischer Gastfreundschaft ausmacht. Ein weiterer Höhepunkt ist der ganz in zartem Grün und gebrochenem Weiß gehaltene Six Senses Spa mit seinen 28 freistehenden Behandlungsstudios, umgeben von blühenden Gärten und Wasserwegen, die größte Wellnessanlage im Mittleren Osten. Ein völlig von der Öffentlichkeit abgeschirmter Teil ist – ganz arabische Tradition – ausschließlich Frauen vorbehalten.

01 | If you don't want to do without a private pool, you can rent one of the seven Malakiya Villas.

Wer auf seinen privaten Pool nicht verzichten will, kann sich in eine der sieben Malakiya Villen einmieten.

02 | The panorama view illustrates the scale and the diversity of this setting. The stilt houses to the left in the picture accomodate the Pierchic fish restaurant. Clearly visible in the background is the Burj Al Arab, which at 300 meters high is the city's landmark.

Der Panoramablick verdeutlicht die Ausmaße und die Vielfalt dieser Anlage. Die Pfahlbauten links im Bild beherbergen das Fischrestaurant Pierchic, gut sichtbar im Hintergrund ist der Burj Al Arab, das über 300 Meter hohe Wahrzeichen der Stadt.

madinat jumeirah, the arabian resort | 45

01 | Minimalistic, sparingly decorated design characterizes the 105 rooms and 36 Chedi Club suites.

Minimalistisches Design mit sparsam eingesetzten Ornamenten prägt die 105 Zimmer und die 36 Chedi Club Suiten.

the chedi muscat | muscat . oman
DESIGN: Yaya Ibrahim, Jean-Michel Gathy

The area of the resort, which has many wings, is located right by the Gulf of Oman, in the heart of the Sultanate, on the outskirts of the capital of Muscat. The view from this luxurious jewel continues to magically focus on the straits of the Arabian Sea. In the mist towards the East you can sense the former Persian Empire. At the back of the enclosure the Haajjar Mountains and the imposing summit of the Jabal Akhdar soar out of the ground. An entwined system of ponds allure in the inner courtyards, in front of the Chedi Wing is an entire water garden, where palm trees create shadows. You might even think that you are at the Alhambra here, if it wasn't for the modern architecture. Even the personal spaces characterize a seemingly timeless design, which completely stays away from folkloristic echoes, but which consciously incorporates decoration and therefore forms an individual West-Eastern Arabian style. Oriental flair is conveyed in the lobby, lounge and restaurant. Arches and countless light sources paint a picture of 1001 Nights, framed by wooden decks and beams. Nevertheless: at the end is this view of the rippling, yet azure blue sea, which is especially captivating. Sitting in the deep armchairs of the Cabanas by the pool, you can gaze lost in thought at the vista. After pure relaxation in the spa and hours spent on the hotel beach, thoughts start to turn towards the selection of Mediterranean and Asian menus in the restaurant. Which wine will be the perfect match?

Das mit vielen Gebäudeflügeln versehene Gelände des Resorts liegt unmittelbar am Golf von Oman, im Herzen des Sultanats, am Rande der Hauptstadt Muskat. Der Blick in diesem luxuriösen Kleinod heftet sich immer wieder wie magisch angezogen auf die Meerenge des Arabischen Meeres. Im Dunst gen Osten erahnt man das ehemalige Persische Reich. Im Rücken der Anlage erheben sich das Hajar-Gebirge und die imposanten Gipfel des Jabal Akhdar. In die Innenhöfe lockt ein verschlungenes System von Teichen, vor dem Chedi Wing liegt gar ein ganzer Wassergarten. Palmen spenden dazu Schatten. So manches Mal mag man sich hier an die Alhambra erinnert fühlen, wäre da nicht die moderne Architektur. Gerade die persönlichen Räume prägen ein zeitlos anmutendes Design, das sich von folkloristischen Anklängen ganz und gar fern hält, Ornamente aber sehr bewusst einsetzt und damit einen eigenen west-östlich-arabischen Stil bildet. Orientalisches Flair vermitteln Lobby, Lounge und Restaurant. Zipfelbögen und zahllose Lichtquellen malen ein Tausendundeine Nacht-Ambiente, von Holzdecken und Balken umrahmt. Nichtsdestotrotz: Am Ende ist es diese Sicht auf das immer wieder krause, gleichwohl azurblaue Meer, das besonders gefangen nimmt. Man sitzt in den tiefen Sesseln der Cabanas am Pool und streift versonnen mit seinen Augen umher. Nach purer Erholung in der Spa und Stunden am hauseigenen Strand richten sich die Gedanken bereits auf die Auswahl unter den mediterranen und asiatischen Menüs im Restaurant. Welcher gute Tropfen mag dazu passen?

02 | From your private bathroom to the pools, ponds and water gardens to the ocean; everything here, is geared towards well-being and water.

Alles ist hier auf Wellness und Wasser ausgerichtet. Vom eigenen Bad über die Pools, Teiche und Wassergärten bis hin zum Meer.

03 | The Gulf of Oman stretches out right on the hotel's doorstep.

Direkt vor der Haustür erstreckt sich der Golf von Oman.

03

04 | 05 | 06 It is the successful fusion of East and West, which defines the cosmopolitan character of the hotel, whether it be in the lobby, guest rooms or spa.

Es ist die gelungene Verbindung von Orient und Okzident, die den kosmopolitischen Charakter des Hotels bestimmt. Sei dies in der Lobby, den Gästezimmern oder im Spa.

the chedi muscat | 51

01 | Wind and water: The elements are omnipresent at the Constance Belle Mare Plage.

Wind und Wasser: Im Constance Belle Mare Plage sind die Elemente allgegenwärtig.

constance belle mare plage | poste de flacq . mauritius
DESIGN: Jean-Marc Eynaud, Martin Branner, Colin Okashimo

There is truly no lack of beautiful beaches in Mauritius—but this one falls into the category of "picture book scenery": One mile long, lined with palm trees, powder white sands and located right on the Indian Ocean, where the turquoise blue shines so brilliantly, it's as if someone has turned on underwater flood lights. The hotel, which adjoins this paradise, is the Constance Belle Mare Plage—famous amongst golfers for its two 18-hole courses, but is also one of the best addresses on the island for connoisseurs and design fans. Architect Jean-Marc Eynaud has integrated the straw-covered buildings of the five star resort extraordinarily easily into the tropical landscape; space, expanse and water are omnipresent and the rooms and suites are cool, yet not cold. Famous guests and anyone yearning for total privacy will find their "home away from home" in one of the 21 villas—the dream vacation homes indulge guests with luxurious interiors, a private pool and a personal butler, who really will fulfill every wish; everything from a breakfast of exotic fruits to a candlelight dinner under the stars. Even laying out fresh towels on the sun lounger, serving you ice cold refresher wipes or cleaning your sunglasses are part of his repertoire.

An schönen Stränden herrscht auf Mauritius wahrlich kein Mangel – doch dieser fällt in die Kategorie „Bilderbuchkulisse": Zwei Kilometer lang, von Palmen gesäumt, mit weißem Puderzuckersand und direkt am Indischen Ozean, dessen Türkisblau hier so intensiv leuchten kann, als habe jemand unter Wasser Scheinwerfer angeschaltet. Das Hotel, das an dieses Paradies grenzt, ist das Constance Belle Mare Plage – bei Golfern dank seiner zwei 18-Loch-Plätze berühmt, aber auch für Ästheten und Designfans eine der besten Adressen der Insel. Architekt Jean-Marc Eynaud hat die strohgedeckten Gebäude des 5-Sterne-Resorts außergewöhnlich leicht in die tropische Landschaft gesetzt; Raum, Weite und Wasser sind allgegenwärtig, und die Zimmer und Suiten geben sich cool, aber nicht kühl. Prominente Gäste und alle, die sich nach Privatsphäre pur sehnen, finden in einer der 21 Villen ihr „home away from home" – die Traumhäuser auf Zeit verwöhnen mit luxuriösen Interieurs, einem privaten Pool und einem persönlichen Butler, der vom Frühstück mit exotischen Früchten bis zum Candle-Light-Dinner unter den Sternen wirklich jeden Wunsch erfüllt. Sogar das Ausbreiten der Badetücher auf der Sonnenliege, das „Servieren" eisgekühlter Erfrischungstücher oder das Reinigen der Sonnenbrille gehört zu seinem Repertoire.

02 | The huge main pool on two levels has the effect of a piazza made of water. On the right is the bar, on the left the restaurant.

Der riesige Hauptpool auf zwei Ebenen wirkt wie eine Piazza aus Wasser. Rechts befindet sich die Bar, links das Restaurant.

03 | 04 Pure design with an Asian influence turns the rooms into little paradises. The 21 villas of the resort will mesmerize you with their own pools and complete privacy.

Schlichtes Design mit asiatischem Einfluss macht die Zimmer zu kleinen Paradiesen. Die 21 Villen des Resorts faszinieren mit eigenen Pools und Privatsphäre pur.

taj exotica resort & spa | wolmar . mauritius
DESIGN: Maurice Giraud Architects, David Edwards/James Park Associates

A large number of the over one million residents live in the west of the island. Despite the relatively dense colonization and a coastal strip lined with resorts, the beaches are more peaceful. This especially applies to the Taj Exotica Resort & Spa, which only opened in 2004. Although situated on the edge of the rather busy fisherman's village of Wolmar, only the souvenir sellers or boat hirers on the beach remind you that you have not been left completely alone on this island. As the only resort in Mauritius, the Taj Exotica only has villas with private pools; there are over 65, which are distributed throughout the 21 acres tropical park. From the armchairs and chaise longues on your own terrace you can enjoy more views of the sea, the Mauritius typical mountains and the coral reef, which surrounds the island. Grand scale is not the term to describe this resort. Everything is huge, from the bathrooms and their open air showers, to the bedrooms, the doors which open to merge with the terraces and private pools to create a large indoor and outdoor living space. The visually most attractive and cozy areas are however the contemporary design restaurant, café and lounge, which are grouped around the main pool down to the beach. The Jiva Spa, which combines Ayurveda and Western treatments on over 21,500 square feet, also receives the best reviews.

Von den über einer Million Einwohnern lebt ein Großteil im Westen der Insel. Trotz der relativ dichten Besiedlung und einem von Resorts besäumten Küstenstreifen, ist es an den Stränden eher ruhig. Ganz besonders gilt das für das erst 2004 eröffnete Taj Exotica Resort & Spa. Obwohl am Rande des eher umtriebigen Fischerörtchens Wolmar gelegen, sind es nur die Souvenirverkäufer oder Bootsverleiher am Strand, die einen daran erinnern, nicht alleine auf einer Insel zurückgelassen worden zu sein. Als einziges Resort auf Mauritius hat das Taj Exotica ausschließlich Villen mit privaten Pools. 65 an der Zahl und die verteilen sich auf einem elf Hektar großen tropischen Park. Aus den Sesseln und Chaiselongues auf der eigenen Terrasse bietet sich ein weiter Blick auf das Meer, die für Mauritius typischen spitzen Berge und auf das Korallenriff, das die Insel umgibt. Großzügigkeit ist hier keine Floskel. Alles ist ein wenig Jumbo. Angefangen von den Bädern mit ihren Freiluftduschen bis zu den Schlafzimmern, die bei geöffneten Türen mit den Terrassen und Privatpools zu einem großen Innen-Außenwohnraum verschmelzen. Zum optisch reizvollsten und gemütlichsten zählen jedoch Restaurant, Café und Lounge, die sich in zeitgenössischem Design gestaltet um den Hauptpool herum zum Strand hin gruppieren. Beste Kritiken erhält auch das Jiva Spa, das auf 2000 Quadratmetern ayurvedische und westliche Behandlungen kombiniert.

01 | "Big" is the buzzword here. These king size mattresses around the swimming pool–in earshot of the "Breakers" bar and lounge–are the perfect place to let your mind wander.

Die Zeichen stehen hier auf „groß". Um das Schwimmbad herum - in Rufweite zur „Breakers" Bar und Lounge - laden diese Kingsize-Matratzen zum Abschalten ein.

02 | 03 Two restaurants and the bar with a lounge can be found around the resort's pool, each with smooth transitions from inside to outside.

Um den Resortpool herum befinden sich zwei Restaurants sowie die Bar mit Lounge, jeweils mit fließenden Übergängen zwischen innen und außen.

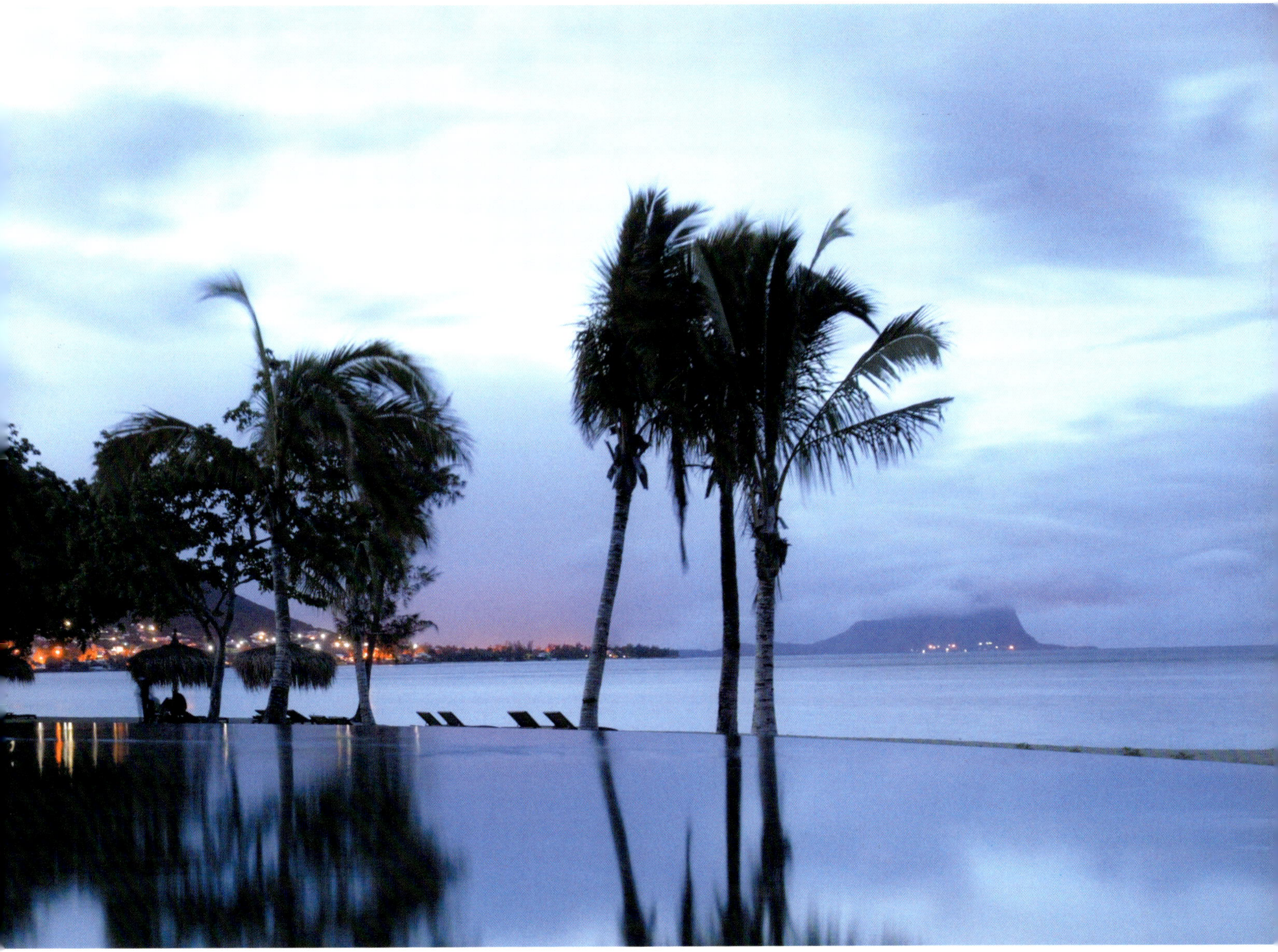

north island | north island . seychelles
DESIGN: LIFE, Silvio Rech & Lesley Carstens

Without a doubt, North Island is one of those once-in-a-lifetime experiences that are well worth saving for. Architects and designers Silvio Rech and Lesley Carstens have created a brilliant fusion of ethnic style and meditative purism—natural wood floors, plump upholstery, a sea of plush cushions and contemporary designer furniture. There is a pool hewn into the rock and a minimalist, mirror-like water channel. None of this would have been possible without the visionary Wilderness Safaris and a group of like-minded people. They bought up the entire island and built eleven guest villas, each at least 4,8 square feet. North Island is around 15 minutes from Mahé by helicopter and at a distance of a few hundred meters the island appears almost uninhabited. It is their intention to keep it that way—unspoilt and rich in plant and animal life. They even decided against a jetty, maintaining it would spoil the view and be just too convenient. Guests going on a trip by boat have to wade the last few miles through emerald-green waters on soft, velvety sand, with relaxation mode kicking in, if it hasn't done so already.

Zweifellos, diese Adresse zählt zu den „Einmal-im-Leben-Geschenken", für die es sich lohnt zu sparen. Virtuos hat es das Architekten- und Designerpaar Silvio Rech und Lesley Carstens verstanden, urige Gemütlichkeit und meditativen Purismus zu kombinieren. Hier ein Boden mit sägerauen Dielen, dazwischen dicke Polster und ein Meer aus plüschigen Kissen, darauf modernes Architekten-Mobiliar. Hier ein in den Fels gehauener Pool, dort ein minimalistischer, spiegelglatter Wasserkanal. Ermöglicht hat dies eine von Visionen beseelte Eignergruppe um Wilderness Safaris. Sie kauften die gesamte Insel, die rund 15 Helikopterminuten entfernt von Mahé liegt und statteten sie mit elf Gästevillen aus, von denen jede mindestens 450 Quadratmeter groß ist. Bei so dünner Population wirkt die Insel aus ein paar hundert Metern Entfernung fast unbewohnt. Ganz im Sinne der Eignergruppe, die die Ursprünglichkeit der Insel mit all ihren Pflanzen- und Tierarten erhalten möchte. Sogar auf einen Bootsanlegesteg hat man verzichtet. „Stört die Optik und macht bequem". Wer mit dem Boot Ausflüge macht, darf deshalb die letzten paar Meter durch das smaragdgrüne Wasser auf weichem Sand waten. Spätestens dabei wird die innere Uhr auf Entspannung geschaltet.

01 | Plunge pool with sala.
Plungepool mit Sala.

02 | The resort contributes to the preservation of a unique natural environment—and offers the greatest possible seclusion at the same time.

Das Resort trägt zum Erhalt einer einzigartigen Natur bei – und bietet gleichzeitig eine größtmögliche Abgeschiedenheit.

03 | A curtain of coral: the screen to protect you from the sun on the private spa table built in echt villa.

Ein Korallenvorhang als Abschirmung gegen die Sonne im privaten Spa-Bereich jeder Villa.

04 | The main piazza: architecture in harmony with nature.

Im Aufenthaltsbereich: Architektur im Einklang mit der Natur.

05 | Lounge area in one of the island's eleven villas.

Lounge-Bereich in einer der elf Villen der Insel.

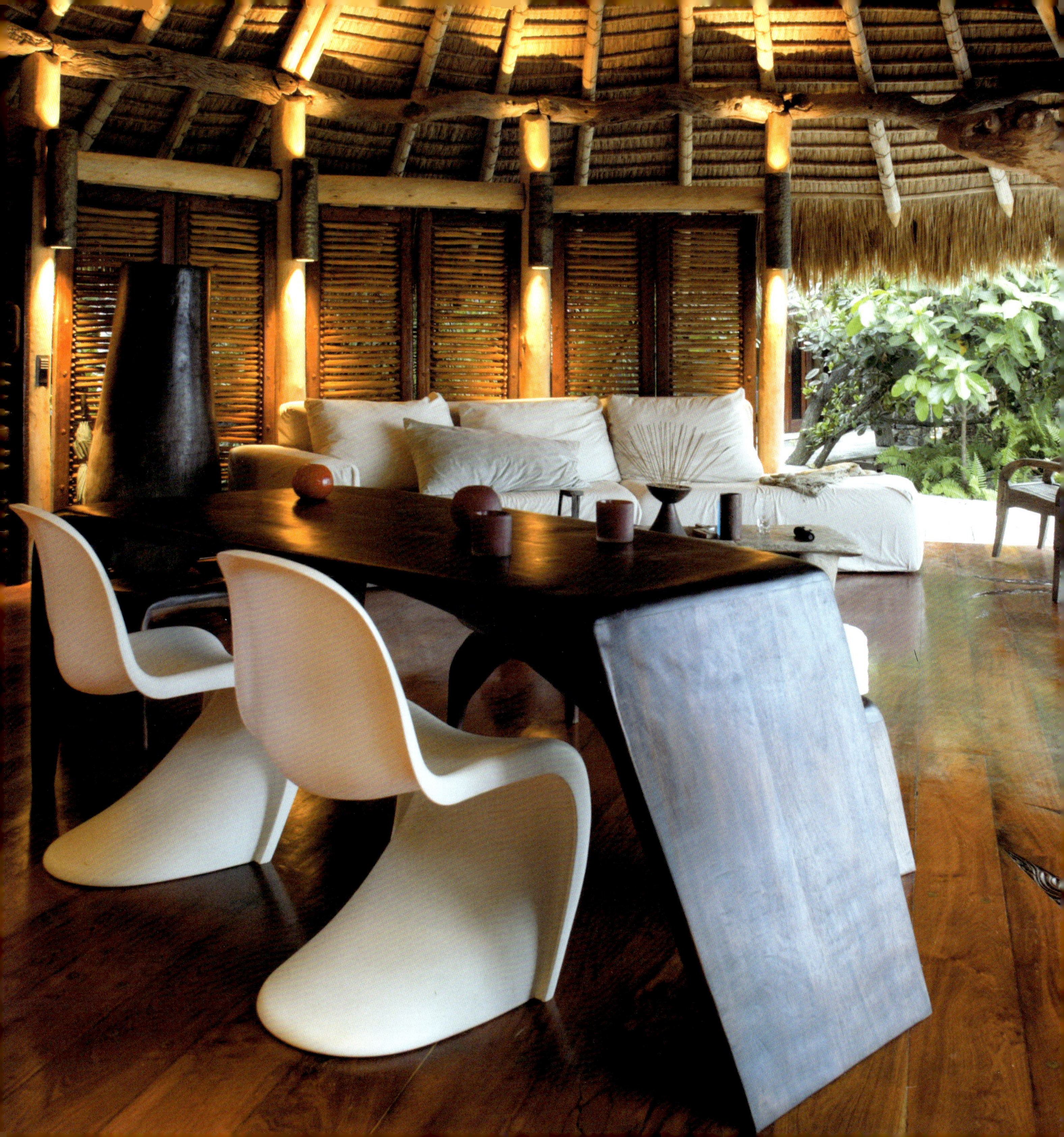

01 | Dreaming under white veils: four-poster bed with mosquito net.
Träumen unter weißem Schleier: Himmelbett mit Moskitonetz.

alfajiri villas | diani beach . kenya
DESIGN: Marika Molinaro

The constant splashing of the Indian Ocean, one of the gentlest rhythms of Africa, lulls guests to sleep in the evening. And if the windows of the Beach Villa are left open at night the rush of the sea can also be heard. Under the white mosquito nets, which overstretch king size beds, you will dream of lions and elephants. Many Africans believe the Alfajiri villas on the south coast of Kenya to be one of the most beautiful and stylishly luxurious hideaways on the East African coast. Which is not particularly surprising considering that the owners are Italian. With a confidently stylish taste the European proprietors have decorated the guest rooms with handicrafts, sculptures and fabrics from Africa and the Far East. Carved doors from Lamu lead to the Cliff, Garden and Beach Villas and roofs built in a high Makuti style. Most of the furniture was made in the on-site workshops. Also contributing to the ambience is the Diani Beach, with its fine powdery sand, where the three villas take front row seats. The guests can enjoy fantastic views over the ocean from almost every corner of the hotel. Summer houses, home-grown palm trees and the turquoise green glittering pool provide a refreshing experience in the garden.

Das gleichmäßige Schnauben des Indischen Ozeans, einer der zärtlichsten Rhythmen von Afrika, wiegt die Gäste abends in den Schlaf. Bei offenem Fenster ist in der Beach Villa auch nachts noch das Rauschen des Meeres zu hören. Unter den weißen Moskitonetzen, die die Kingsize-Betten überspannen, lässt es sich von Löwen und Elefanten träumen. Viele Afrikaner halten die Alfajiri Villen an der Südküste Kenias für eines der schönsten und stilvollsten Luxusrefugien der ostafrikanischen Küste. Was angesichts der Nationalität der italienischen Besitzer nicht besonders überrascht. Mit stilsicherem Geschmack haben die europäischen Eigentümer die Gästezimmer mit Kunsthandwerk, Skulpturen und Stoffen aus Afrika und dem Fernen Osten eingerichtet. Geschnitzte Türen aus Lamu führen in die Cliff, Garden und Beach Villa, deren Dächer im hohen Makuti-Stil gebaut sind. Die meisten Möbel wurden in den hauseigenen Werkstätten hergestellt. Zum Ambiente trägt auch der feinpudrige Diani Beach bei, an dem die drei Villen exponierte Logenplätze einnehmen. Die Gäste können von fast jedem Winkel des Hotels aus einen phantastischen Blick auf das Meer genießen. Im Garten sorgen Lauben, selbstgezogene Palmen und der türkisgrün glitzernde Pool für Frische.

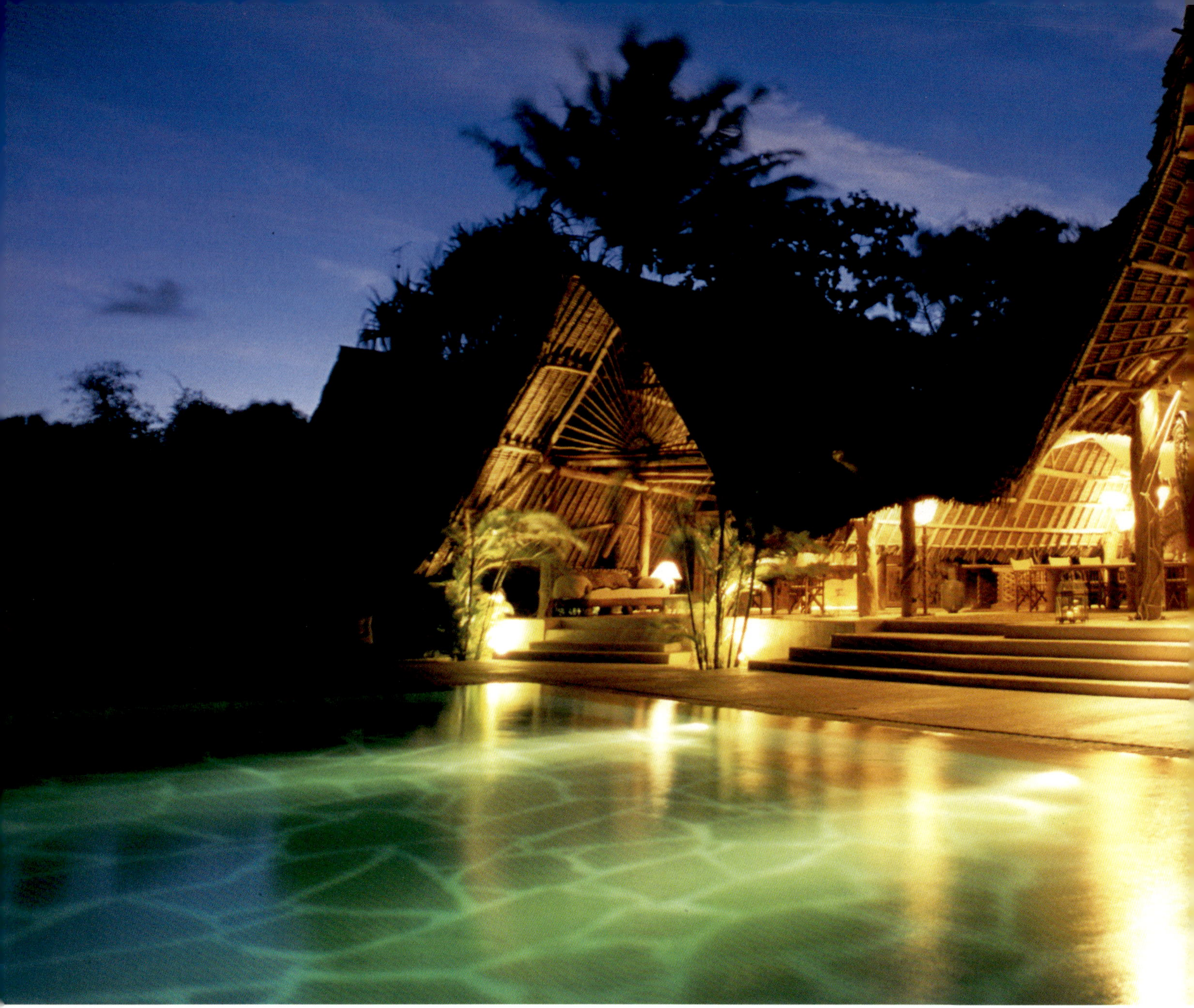

02 | The high roofs are constructed in Makuti style.
Die hohen Dächer sind im Makuti-Stil errichtet.

03 | The pool and sandy beach are both as equally enticing for swimmers.
Zum Baden locken Pool und Sandstrand gleichermaßen.

alfajiri villas | 67

matemo island resort | quirimbas archipel . mozambique
DESIGN: RSL, Nikki McCarthy Interiors

It is regarded as one of the most beautiful diving and fishing territories in the world: the small island of Matemo, one of 36 nearly pristine islands in the Quirimbas Archipelago off the north east coast of Mozambique. Here, situated directly on the white, fine sandy beach, is the "Matemo Island Resort". Designed in an ethnic style with Portuguese, Arabic and African elements, the hotel accommodates 24 luxurious beach chalets. Guests have a panoramic view of the sea and the lush palm trees. Every chalet has a large veranda with hammock and loungers, as well as direct access to the beach. Refreshment is provided either in the hotel swimming pool or the crystal clear, turquoise colored Indian Ocean, where swimming is possible all-year round. The hotel is also a diving base and offers daily water sport and excursion options—from water skiing and kayaking to open sea fishing through to sailing trips at sunset. Of particular appeal is diving to the coral reefs with their rich animal kingdom. Particularly suitable are the months of August to November, when humpback whales can be observed off Matemo.

Es gilt als eines der schönsten Tauch- und Angelreviere der Welt: Das kleine Eiland Matemo, eine von 36 nahezu unberührten Inseln im Quirimbas-Archipel vor der Nordostküste Mosambiks. Hier, unmittelbar am weißen, feinsandigen Sandstrand gelegen, befindet sich das Matemo Island Resort. Im ethnischen Stil mit portugiesischen, arabischen und afrikanischen Elementen gestaltet, beherbergt das Hotel 24 luxuriöse Strandchalets. Dem Gast bietet sich ein Panoramablick auf das Meer sowie auf üppige Palmenhaine. Jedes Chalet verfügt über eine große Veranda mit Hängematte sowie Liegestühlen und besitzt direkten Zugang zum Strand. Für eine Erfrischung sorgen entweder der Hotel-Swimmingpool oder der kristallklare, türkisfarbene Indische Ozean, der ganzjährig zum Baden einlädt. Das Hotel dient auch als Tauchbasis und offeriert täglich Wassersport- und Ausflugsmöglichkeiten – angefangen von Wasserski und Kajakfahren über Hochseeangeln bis hin zu Segeltörns bei Sonnenuntergang. Von besonderem Reiz sind Tauchgänge in den Korallenriffen mit ihrer reichen Tierwelt. Die Monate August bis November eignen sich zudem besonders gut, weil dort vor Matemo Buckelwale zu beobachten sind.

01 | The pool and poolbar under a palm tree roof can be found right by the sea.

Pool und Poolbar unterm Palmendach befinden sich direkt am Meer.

02 | The half a mile long, white beach stretches right along the hotel.

Unmittelbar vor dem Hotel erstreckt sich der kilometerlange, weiße Strand.

03 | The beach chalets have been furnished in a Mozambique-typical style with elements made of wood.

Landestypisch wurden die Strandchalets mit vielen Stilelementen aus Holz eingerichtet.

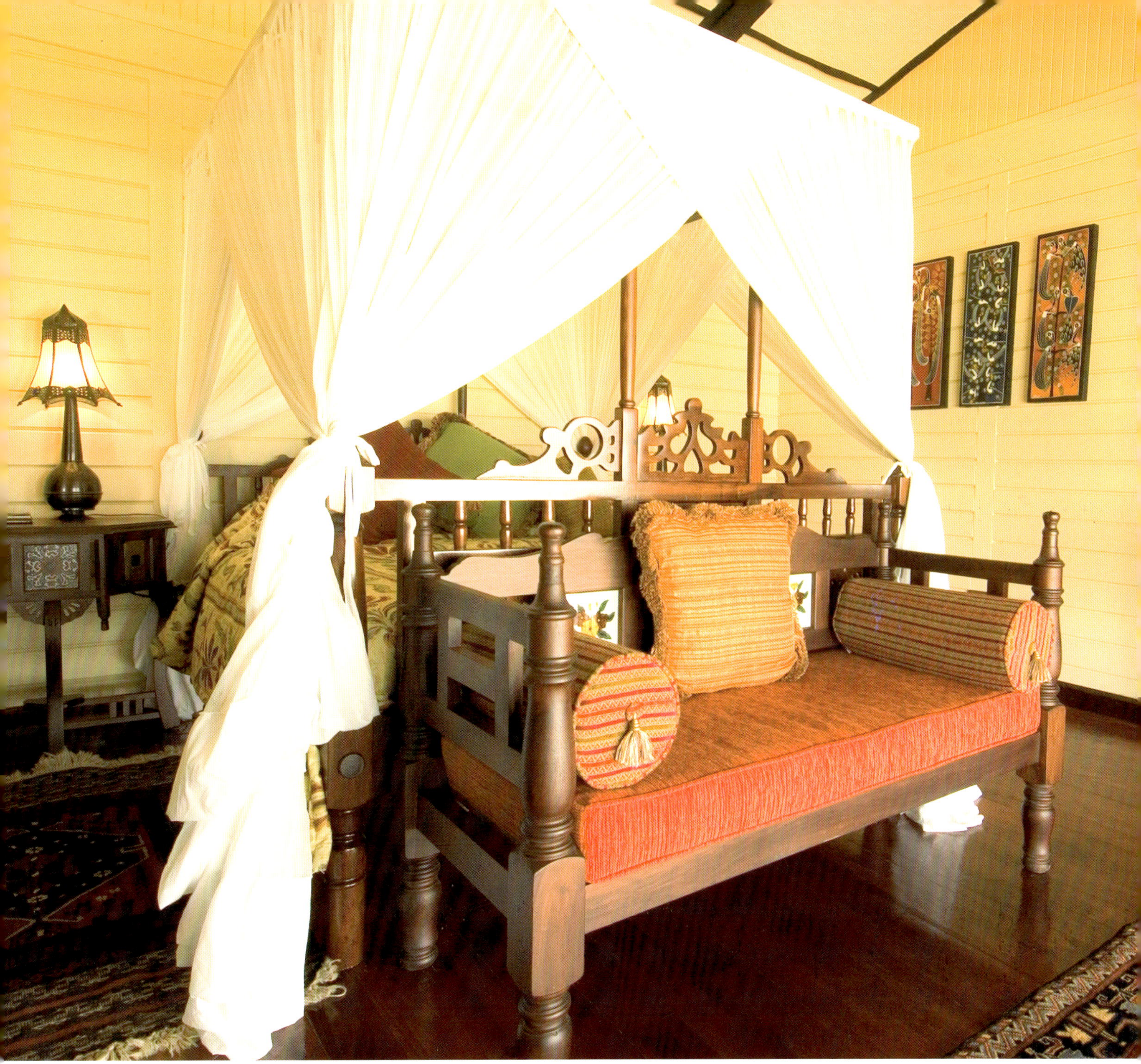

01 | A cream hotel above the green coast of the Overberg.
Eine cremfarbene Villa über der grünen Küste des Overberg.

birkenhead house | hermanus . south africa
DESIGN: Liz Biden and Ralph Krall, Phil Biden and Michael Dall

Whale watching from your sun lounger: when hundreds of Southern Right whales move from the Antarctic to the South African coast between July and November to give birth to their offspring in the bays of Hermanus, no front row seat is more stylish than the pool terrace of Birkenhead House. The boutique hotel thrones on a cliff over "Walker-Bay", from where the fountain spouting sea mammals can be observed up close and personal. The elegant shell tones of the house, dazzling white and cream-colored vanilla, act as a contrast to the green of the landscape. American shutters filter the reflecting light from the sea. The nostalgic bathrooms and rooms are furnished with an eclectic mix of antique and modern. If the pool in the inner courtyard is not refreshing enough for you, then venture down a few steps to the beach and into the waves of the Indian Ocean. And in the evening, when the humped backs of the whales disappear into the twilight and the lanterns are lit on the patio, it's time to enjoy the seafood on your plate. The young team serves several course gourmet menus with freshly-caught fish, lobster and sushi and top class South African house wine. All meals and local beverages are included in the price.

Vom Liegestuhl aus Wale beobachten: Wenn zwischen Juli und November Hunderte von Südlichen Glattwalen von der Antarktis zur südafrikanischen Küste ziehen, um in den Buchten vor Hermanus ihre Jungen zur Welt zu bringen, dann gibt es keinen stilvolleren Logenplatz als die Pool-Terrasse des Birkenhead House. Das exponiert gelegene Boutique-Hotel thront auf einer Klippe über der „Walker-Bay", von der aus sich die fontänespeienden Meeressäuger aus der Nähe betrachten lassen. Die eleganten Muscheltöne des Hauses, leuchtendes Weiß und cremefarbene Vanille, heben sich vom Grün der Landschaft ab. Hohe Fensterläden filtern das vom Meer reflektierende Licht. Die nostalgischen Bäder und Zimmer sind mit Antiquitäten und im modernen Stil ausgestattet. Wem der Pool im Innenhof zur Erfrischung nicht ausreicht, der wagt sich am nur ein paar Treppenstufen entfernten Badestrand in die Wellen des Indischen Ozeans. Abends, wenn die buckeligen Rücken der Wale in der Dämmerung verschwinden und die Laternen im Patio angezündet werden, kann man dann die Früchte des Meeres auf dem Teller genießen. Das junge Team serviert mehrgängige Gourmetmenüs mit fangfrischem Fisch, Hummer sowie Sushi und südafrikanischen Hauswein der Spitzenklasse. Alles ist im Preis inklusive.

74 | birkenhead house

02 | The fireplace in the card room.

Ein offener Kamin im Kartenzimmer.

03 | The calm before the bath: the chaise longue in front of the bathtub is the perfect place for stylish lounging.

Die Ruhe vor dem Bad: Die Chaiselongue vor der Wanne lädt zum stilvollen Lümmeln ein.

04 | The columns give Birkenhead House a noble flair.

Die Säulen verleihen Birkenhead House ein nobles Flair.

76 | birkenhead house

05 | Dreaming in white-gold: the bedroom is decorated in a sensuous, airy style.

Träumen in Weiß-Gold: Das Schlafzimmer ist in einem sinnlich-luftigen Stil eingerichtet.

06 | The boutique hotel is divided between three buildings. To the left of the pool in the inner courtyard is a small bar and card room. In pleasant weather the glass panel is opened.

Das Boutique-Hotel verteilt sich über drei Gebäude. Links vom Pool im Innenhof befinden sich eine kleine Bar und der Kartenraum. Bei angenehmem Klima ist die Glaswand geöffnet.

01 | Since 2005 there has also been two Amanresorts in Sri Lanka, both in Galle; the Amangalla in a 400 year old Galle Fort and the Amanwella right by the beach.

Seit 2005 gibt es auch in Sri Lanka zwei Amanresorts, beide in Galle, das Amangalla im 400 Jahre alten Galle Fort und das Amanwella direkt am Strand.

amanwella | tangalle . sri lanka
DESIGN: Kerry Hill

In 2005 Amanresorts opened two hotels in the South of Sri Lanka, one of them right on the "golden" beach. Inner calm and peace muss will be bestowed on those who eavesdrop on the waves of the Indian Ocean from the private terraces of one of the 30 suites. Romantic strolls under coconut palms, rejuvenating massages in the hotel spa and a cool drink by the pool take it that one step further. However the sea itself is only peaceful in the winter months on the rough south coast of the island, during the drought. Due to the high waves in the summer you're better off relocating the swimming to the 150 foot-long pool. If it's total privacy you desire, you can paddle in one of the bathing pools, which can be found in every suite. A completely uninterrupted sea view is offered by the suites right on the beach. If it's solitude you're looking for then you can reserve a secluded villa, in the hills of the hideaway. But of course also here you will enjoy views of the sea and the grove of coconut palms. The architect and designer Kerry Hill, has mainly combined the country's traditional materials in Amanwella. Used in the construction were for example old terracotta, roof tiles, hand-cut stones and lots of wood.

Amanresorts haben 2005 gleich zwei Hotels im Süden von Sri Lanka eröffnet, eines davon direkt an dem „goldenen" Strand. Innere Ruhe und Frieden muss einfach finden, wer von der privaten Terrasse einer der 30 Suiten den Wogen des Indischen Ozeans lauscht. Romantische Spaziergänge unter Kokospalmen, Wohlfühlmassagen im hoteleigenen Spa und ein kühler Drink am Pool tun ihr Übriges. Richtig friedlich ist das Meer, selbst an der rauen Südküste der Insel, allerdings nur in den Wintermonaten, während der Trockenzeit. Im Sommer verlegt man das Schwimmen wegen des hohen Wellengangs besser in den 45 Meter langen Pool. Wer es ganz privat mag, planscht in einem der Bassins, das zu jeder Suite gehört. Einen gänzlich unverstellten Blick auf die See bieten die Suiten direkt am Strand. Abgeschiedenheit findet, wer sich eine Villa abseits, in den Hügeln der Anlage reserviert. Aber auch hier natürlich mit Blick aufs Meer und den Hain aus Kokospalmen. Der Architekt und Designer Kerry Hill kombinierte im Amanwella hauptsächlich traditionelle Materialien des Landes. Für den Bau wurden beispielsweise alte Dachziegel aus Terrakotta, handbehauene Steine und sehr viel Holz verwendet.

02 | All 30 suites have the same layout and design. Their only difference is in the location.

Alle 30 Suiten sind gleich in Grundriss und Design. Sie unterscheiden sich lediglich in ihrer Lage.

03 | Visit the library to find out about the history, art, culture and animal kingdom of Sri Lanka.

Die Bücherei informiert über Geschichte, Kunst, Kultur und Tierwelt von Sri Lanka.

04 | An amble along the village of Wella Wathura also leads through the jungle. If you pay attention you'll spot monkeys, lizards and mongooses.

Ein Spaziergang am Dorf Wella Wathura entlang führt auch durch den Dschungel. Wer genau aufpasst, begegnet Affen, Waranen und Mungos.

04

saman villas | bentota . sri lanka
DESIGN: Geevaka de Soyza, Murad Ismail

Beruwela is on one of the most beautiful sections of coast, located in the south-west of Sri Lanka. As a result it is also one of the areas with the highest density of hotels. The Saman Villas are somewhat secluded from the touristy hustle and bustle perched on a rocky headland. To the left and right hand are miles of coconut plantation-lined sandy beaches. The grounds are exclusive; with only 26 suites and one villa, where mostly only two of which can be found in one building, give the resort a deserted feeling, even when it's fully occupied. All rooms are decorated in the grand scale layout and the country-typical style of the island with colored embroidered silk scarves, high-grade woods and wooden carvings. The architecture is suited to the climate conditions with sliding walls, gardens with water basins and water channels, interrupted by islands with tropical plants. A pavilion in the center of a water square, a wooden terrace built onto the cliff or seating between water, stone and vegetation turn nature into a living space. This also conforms to the newly added Sahama Spa, which was designed as a Far East garden setting, plus the swimming pool set into a rock formation, the edge of which seems to seamlessly merge into the sea and where the roar of the surf can be heard as if you were swimming in the ocean yourself. One of the most inspiring places is the library with its wooden paneling in an English colonial style. From here, you can be transported to far off places, whether it's by reading a book, glancing out over the ocean or observing the sky through a telescope.

Beruwela im Südwesten Sri Lankas liegt an einem der schönsten Küstenabschnitte. Folglich ist es auch eines der Gebiete mit der höchsten Hoteldichte. Die Saman Villas thronen jedoch etwas abseits vom touristischen Trubel an exponierter Stelle auf einem Felsvorsprung. Rechts und links davon sind kilometerlange von Kokosplantagen gesäumte Sandstrände. Die Anlage präsentiert sich exklusiv. Bei nur 26 Suiten und einer Villa, die sich meist paarweise ein eigenes Gebäude teilen, wirkt das Resort selbst bei voller Belegung noch menschenleer. Alle Zimmer sind von großzügigem Zuschnitt und im landestypischen Stil der Insel eingerichtet mit farbig bestickten Seidentüchern, Edelhölzern und Holzschnitzereien. Den klimatischen Bedingungen Rechnung trägt die Architektur mit geöffneten Wänden, Gärten mit Wasserbecken und Wasserrinnen, unterbrochen von Inseln mit tropischer Bepflanzung. Ein Pavillon inmitten eines Wasserquadrats, eine auf den Felsen gebaute Holzterrasse oder Sitzgelegenheiten zwischen Wasser, Stein und Vegetation lassen Natur zum Lebensraum werden. Dem entspricht auch das neu hinzugefügte, als fernöstliche Gartenanlage konzipierte Sahama Spa sowie das den Felsformationen angepasste Schwimmbad. Dessen Rand geht optisch nahtlos in den Ozean über und man hört die Brandung, als ob man selbst im Meer schwimmen würde. Einer der inspirierendsten Orte ist die Bibliothek mit Holztäfelung im englischen Kolonialstil. Von hier aus kann man gleich in mehrfacher Hinsicht in die Ferne schweifen, sei es beim Lesen eines Buches, beim Blick aufs Meer oder per Teleskop ins Firmament.

01 | The Sahama Spa in a Far Eastern garden setting.
Das Sahama-Spa in einer fernöstlichen Gartenanlage.

02 03
04

02 | View from the sun lounger over the swimming pool to the coconut tree-lined coast.

Blick von der Liegeterrasse über den Swimmingpool auf die mit Kokospalmen gesäumte Küstenlinie.

03 | The open inner courtyard of the Sahama Spa is designed as a water garden.

Der offene Innenhof des Sahama Spas ist als Wassergarten angelegt.

04 | 05 The suites have a minimalistic look, but with noble furnishings.

In minimalistischer Optik, aber edler Ausstattung, präsentieren sich die Suiten.

baros maldives | north male atoll . maldives
DESIGN: Mohamed Shafeeg, Anita Indra Dewi

Who knows how many jewels are hidden on the countless islands of the Maldives? It's likely that the approximately 500 miles long beach of coral atolls in the Indian Ocean, south-west of Sri Lanka, is concealing more than just one. The biggest treasures however, are in part still the untouched jewels of nature itself. The strict fishing regulations and the commercial use of the islands is an attempt to maintain the originality of the landscape. Many consist only of small uninhabited sand banks, others stretch for several miles and are covered in lush rainforest. A gem of the Maldives is also the private island of Baros on the North Male Atoll. After the thirty minute journey by speedboat from Male International Airport, you will think you have arrived in a make-believe world. Splashing about in the reefs are parrotfishes, stingrays, turtles and dolphins. Some of the guest houses have been built on stilts directly above the lagoon. Wooden steps lead swimmers and snorkelers straight into the glittering blue water. The very spacious Baros Villas have been built right on the sandy beach. Their terraces reach the water's edge. All buildings are made of original materials like wood and stone, the roofs are made of the foliage from the coconut palms. During the architecture and the construction of the setting, great attention was paid to harmony with the nature and preservation of the habitat.

Wer weiß schon, wie viele Schätze auf den unzähligen Inseln der Malediven versteckt sind? Die etwa 800 Kilometer lange Kette aus Korallenatollen im Indischen Ozean, südwestlich von Sri Lanka hält wahrscheinlich mehr als nur einen verborgen. Die größte Kostbarkeit aber sind die zum Teil noch fast unberührten Schätze der Natur selbst. Die strenge Regulierung der Fischerei und der kommerziellen Nutzung der Inseln versucht die Landschaft in ihrer Ursprünglichkeit zu bewahren. Manche Inseln bestehen lediglich aus kleinen unbewohnten Sandbänken, andere erstrecken sich über mehrere Kilometer und sind üppig mit Regenwald bewachsen. Ein Kleinod der Malediven ist auch die private Insel Baros im Nord-Male-Atoll. Wer nach etwa einer halben Stunde Fahrt mit dem Schnellboot vom Male International Airport ankommt, glaubt sich in einer Traumwelt wiederzufinden. In den Riffs tummeln sich Papageienfische, Stachelrochen, Schildkröten und Delfine. Einige der Gästehäuser wurden auf Pfählen direkt über der Lagune errichtet. Holztreppen führen Schwimmer und Schnorchler geradewegs ins glitzernd blaue Wasser. Die sehr geräumigen Baros-Villen sind unmittelbar auf den Sandstrand gebaut. Ihre Terrassen reichen bis nah ans Wasser. Alle Gebäude bestehen aus ursprünglichen Materialien wie Holz und Stein, die Dächer aus den Blättern der Kokospalme. Bei der Architektur und dem Bau der Anlage wurde vor allem auf die Vereinbarkeit mit der Natur und die Erhaltung des Lebensraums geachtet.

01 | Of the more than 2000 islands and atolls, only 202 are inhabited.
Von den mehr als 2000 Inseln und Atollen sind nur 202 bewohnt.

02
03
04

05

02 | The foliage of the tropical forest provides privacy in the deluxe villas.

Die üppige Vegetation sorgt für Privatsphäre in den Deluxe-Villen.

03 | Baros has a total of 75 villas, on the water, beach and also in the jungle.

Auf Baros stehen insgesamt 75 Villen, sowohl auf dem Wasser, am Strand als auch im Urwald.

04 | The Spa at Baros Maldives offers four spa suites, each with their own private steam room and bathing experience in a tropical garden.

Jede der vier Spa-Suiten auf Baros verfügt über ein privates Dampfbad und ein großzügiges Bad in einem tropischen Garten.

05 | You can get a good overview of the island paradise from a bird's-eye perspective—on a sightseeing flight with the waterplane.

Einen guten Überblick über das Inselparadies erhält man aus der Vogelperspektive – bei einem Rundflug mit dem Wasserflugzeug.

01 | The view from the disco-style illuminated pool to the main house with restaurant, bar and lobby.

Blick vom im Diskostil beleuchteten Pool zum Haupthaus mit Restaurant, Bar und Lobby.

anantara resort maldives | south male atoll . maldives
DESIGN: John Lightbody, Abacus; Mohamed Shafeeg

Tourism in the Maldives is continuing to develop at an almost non-stop pace. And the good news: new projects are more environmentally-conscious and are almost consistently gleaming with attractive architecture. Anantara opened in the South Male Atoll in the late summer of 2006. With Indian influences the planners have combined contemporary Thai design to develop stand-alone island architecture, where water and sand are at the fore. Impressive is the delicate main building made of glass and wood, spectacular is the pool with its cosmological underwater lighting. At sunset the scenery seems almost surreal, especially when the sky turns red like in the photo. All 40 suites are built on stilts in the sea and connected to the land with a wooden pier, the 70 villas are right by the beach. With their reed and palm branch covered roofs, the wide door and window openings and the tropical timber used everywhere for furniture, walls and flooring, plus the cool tiles take into account the temperature. The selection of colors is also attuned to the environment: sand white furniture fabrics, textiles such as cushions and covers as turquoise as the lagoon and little accessories in the pinks and reds of the exotic flora. Four of the suites and houses, which are around 2000 square feet, have their own freshwater pools, as a refreshing alternative to the seawater lagoon. Others have an open air bathtub surrounded by tropical plants and sheltered by a pergola.

Fast ungebremst entwickelt sich der Tourismus auf den Malediven weiter. Die gute Nachricht: Neue Projekte sind umweltbewusster und glänzen fast durchweg mit attraktiver Architektur. So auch das im Spätsommer 2006 eröffnete Anantara im Süd-Male-Atoll. Zeitgenössisches Thai-Design haben die Planer hier mit indischen Einflüssen kombiniert und zur eigenständigen Inselarchitektur entwickelt, bei der Wasser und Sand im Vordergrund stehen. Imposant ist das zierliche Hauptgebäude aus Glas und Holz, spektakulär der Pool mit seiner den Kosmos abbildenden Unterwasserbeleuchtung. Im Abendlicht wirkt die Szenerie geradezu unwirklich. Vor allem dann, wenn sich der Himmel wie auf dem Foto rötet. Alle 40 Suiten sind auf Stelzen ins Meer hinaus gebaut und über einen hölzernen Pier mit dem Land verbunden, die 70 Villen stehen unmittelbar am Strand. Die Schilf und Palmwedel gedeckten Dächer, die weiten Tür- und Fensteröffnungen, die Möbel, Wände und Fußböden aus Tropenholz, sowie die kühlen Kacheln tragen dem Klima Rechnung. Auch die Auswahl der Farben ist auf die Umgebung abgestimmt: sandweiße Möbelstoffe, Wohntextilien wie Kissen und Decken im Türkis der Lagune sowie kleine Accessoires im Pink und Rot der exotischen Flora. Vier der Suiten und die bis zu 180 Quadratmeter großen Häuser verfügen über einen eigenen Süßwasser-Pool, in den man sich als Alternative zur Meerwasser-Lagune erfrischen kann. Andere haben eine von tropischen Pflanzen umsäumte und mit einer Pergola überdachte Freiluft-Badewanne.

02 | The restaurant interior: an airy wooden supporting structure accommodates climatic conditions.

Das Restaurant von innen: Eine luftige Tragwerkkonstruktion aus Holz entspricht den klimatischen Gegebenheiten.

03 | Elegant suites with sophisticated materials, which are attuned to the surroundings.

Elegante Suiten mit edlen Materialien, die auf die Umgebung abgestimmt sind.

04 | Many of the guest houses have their own private "open air pool" amongst the tropical nature.

Viele Gästehäuser verfügen über ein privates „Freibad" in tropischer Natur.

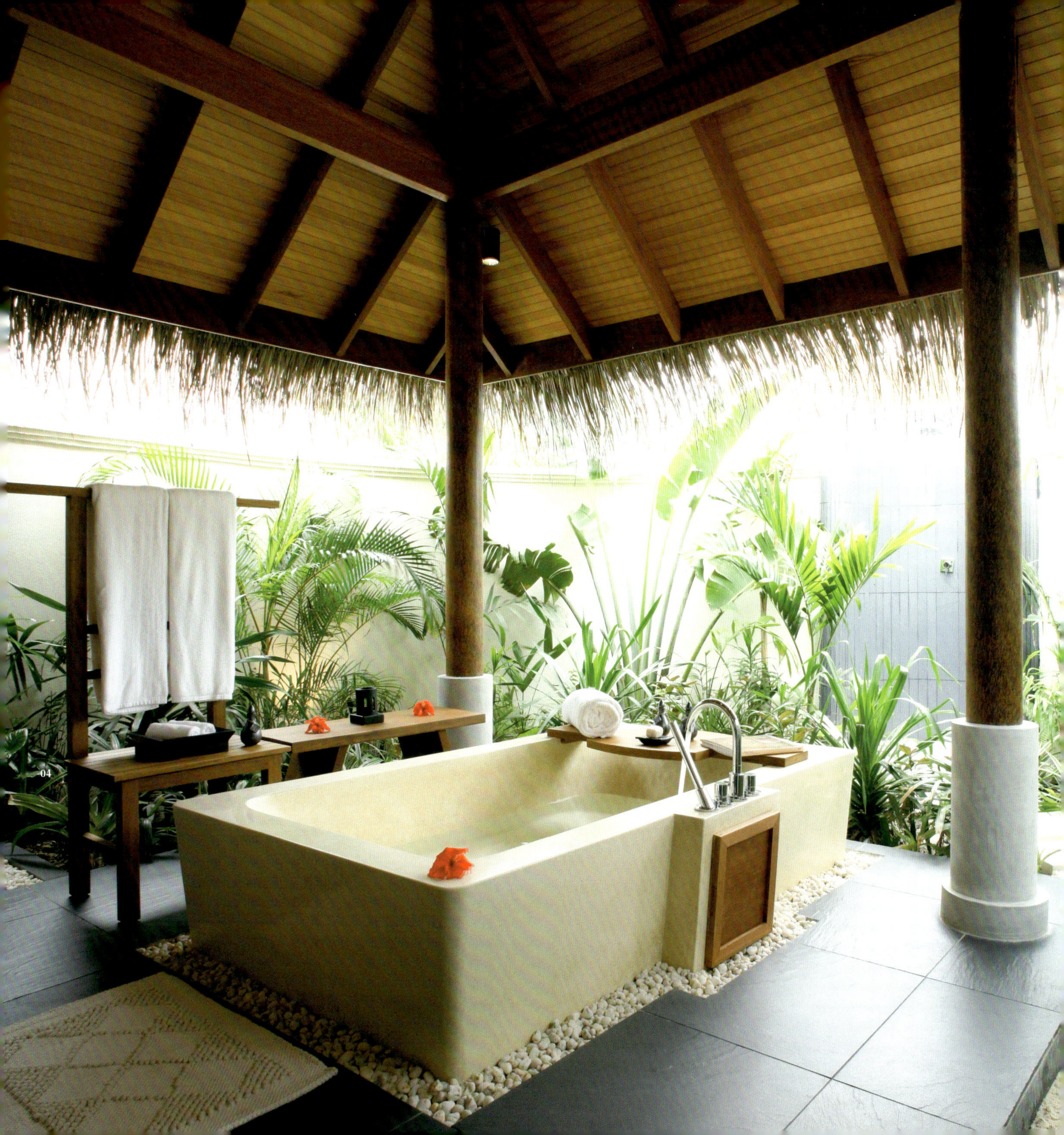
04

01 | The Aleenta Resort and Spa Phuket – Phangnga naturally merges interior and exterior worlds.

Das Aleenta Resort and Spa Phuket – Phangnga verbindet Innen- und Außenwelten wie selbstverständlich.

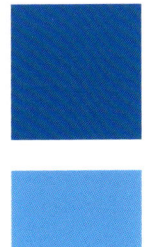

aleenta resort and spa phuket – phangnga | phuket . thailand
DESIGN: Simple Space Design, Shawwah Home Décor

The Natai Beach in Phuket is also known as "the Hamptons of Thailand" In real estate circles—this is where the rich and beautiful build their villas right on the beach of the azure blue Andamanen Sea. If you're not necessarily thinking of settling down on this coastal strip for the rest of your life, but just for a vacation, you'll find your personal paradise at Aleenta Resort and Spa Phuket – Phangnga. The small resort comprises modernly designed suites, lofts and villas, which merge inside and outside living: with subdued colors that pick up on the nuances of nature, an uncomplicated style, which creates never-ending space and expanse, as well as high windows, from which you will look right out onto infinity pools, white beaches and the ocean. The design concept has been thought out down to the very last detail—so for example the fluffy towels and the soft bed linen come from the hotel's own signature series, and pre-programmed iPods provide the befitting musical sounds, which also turn your stay into an acoustic experience. The last hint of stress and worries is massaged away in the spa and you can be indulged in the restaurant with light Thai food. Upon request dinner for two can also be served right on the Natai Beach—and just in case your vacation flirt has turned into a longer relationship after all, it's not too late to contemplate purchasing a home in the Asian Hamptons…

Der Natai Beach auf Phuket wird in Immobilienkreisen auch „die Hamptons von Thailand" genannt – hier bauen die Reichen und Schönen ihre Villen direkt an den Strand der azurblauen Andamanen See. Wer sich an diesem Küstenstreifen nicht gleich fürs ganze Leben, sondern zunächst nur für einen Urlaub niederlassen möchte, findet im Aleenta Resort and Spa Phuket – Phangnga sein persönliches Paradies. Das kleine Resort umfasst modern gestaltete Suiten, Lofts und Villen, die Inside- und Outside-Living miteinander verschmelzen lassen: mit zarten Farben, die Nuancen aus der Natur aufgreifen, schnörkellosem Stil, der unendlichen Raum und Weite schafft, sowie hohen Fensterfronten, aus denen man direkt auf randlose Pools, weiße Strände und den Ozean blickt. Das Designkonzept ist bis ins Detail durchdacht – so stammen zum Beispiel die flauschigen Handtücher und die weiche Bettwäsche aus der hauseigenen Signature-Serie, und für die passenden musikalischen Klänge sorgen vorprogrammierte iPods, die den Aufenthalt auch zu einem akustischen Erlebnis machen. Der letzte Anflug von Stress und Sorgen wird im Spa wegmassiert, und das Restaurant verwöhnt mit leichter thailändischer Kost. Auf Wunsch wird das Dinner for two auch direkt am Natai Beach serviert – und sollte aus dem Ferienflirt dann doch eine längere Beziehung werden, kann man über den Erwerb eines Domizils in den asiatischen Hamptons ja immer noch nachdenken…

02

02 | Living on two floors: a clear design creates space and expanse.
Wohnen auf zwei Ebenen: Klares Design schafft Raum und Weite.

03 | The infinity pools and the Andamanen Sea dazzle in all conceivable tones of blue.
Die randlosen Pools und die Andamanen See leuchten in allen erdenklichen Blautönen.

04 | Even a pool becomes a living space at the Aleenta Resort and Spa Phuket – Phangnga.
Im Aleenta Resort and Spa Phuket – Phangnga wird selbst ein Pool zum Wohnraum.

05 | Bed linen from the Aleenta signature series provide comfort in the bedrooms.
Im Schlafzimmer sorgt Bettwäsche aus der Aleenta Signature-Serie für Komfort.

06 | Twilight shows the suites, lofts and villas in their best light.
Die Dämmerung taucht die Suiten, Lofts und Villen ins beste Licht.

06

01 | Expanding spaces dominate the architecture.
Sich öffnende Räume dominieren die Architektur.

costa lanta | krabi . thailand
DESIGN: Duangrit Bunnag

Lanta Yai is a narrow strip of islands just off Thailand's west coast, not far from Phuket. The beaches are long and stretching, the view to the Indian Ocean restricted and the nature is not yet under threat from urbanization. The beach resort of Costa Lanta pointedly shows this to its best advantage. The setting with its 22 bungalows is imbedded in a landscape similar to a park, with a natural water system running through, over which wooden bridges lead. So that the beach remains a place for everyone, the bungalows were not built right by the sea. The resort wants to offer more than just beach. It focuses vacationers to open their minds to the surrounding nature. Design and interior emphasize this through clear, rhythmic shapes, which concentrate the view of the essence. The "living cubes" are made of polished concrete—a material, which at the same time defines the room atmosphere. The half-open bathrooms with their extra large rain showers and uncomplicated fittings fit in well here. Contrasts are made by the large, low wooden panels, which act as door wings. The minimal furnishings play with wood and light, and fabrics in harmonizing colors—which interact with the design elements to create a modern vanishing point of young elegance and simple privacy.

Lanta Yai ist ein schmaler Inselstreifen vor Thailands Westküste, nur unweit von Phuket. Die Strände sind lang gezogen, der Blick unverstellt auf den Indischen Ozean, die Natur noch nicht von der Verstädterung bedroht. Vorzüge, die das Beach-Resort von Costa Lanta gezielt zur Geltung bringt. Die Anlage mit ihren 22 Bungalowboxen bettet sich in eine parkähnliche Landschaft ein, durchzogen von einem natürlichen Wassersystem. Über sie führen Holzbrücken hinweg. Damit der Strand ein Platz für alle bleibt, platzierte man die Bungalows nicht unmittelbar am Meer. Das Resort will eben mehr bieten als Stranddasein. Es fokussiert Urlauber, deren Seele sich genauso sehr an der umgebenden Natur nährt. Design und Interieur unterstreichen dies durch klare, rhythmisierte Formen, die den Blick auf das Wesentliche konzentrieren. Die Wohnkuben bestehen aus poliertem Beton – ein Material, das zugleich das Raumambiente bestimmt. Die halb offenen Bäder mit ihren extragroßen Regenduschen und schnörkellosen Armaturen fügen sich darin ein. Kontraste setzen große, bodentiefe Holzwände, die als Türflügel fungieren. Das reduzierte Mobiliar spielt mit Holz und hellen, sich farblich harmonisch einfügenden Stoffen – im Zusammenspiel der Designelemente ein moderner Fluchtpunkt von junger Eleganz und schlichter Zurückgezogenheit.

02 | A densely wooded park with waterways and bridges surrounds the resort.
Ein waldreicher Park mit Wasserläufen und Brücken umsäumt das Resort.

03 | Exposed concrete defines the half-open bathroom with extra large rain shower.
Sichtbeton bestimmt das halb offene Bad mit extragroßer Regendusche.

04 | Minimizing the essentials is characteristic of the bungalow atmosphere.
Reduktion auf das Wesentliche prägt das Bungalow-Ambiente.

sala samui resort & spa | koh samui . thailand
DESIGN: Be Gray

Relax under a frangipani tree: situated on the still very much pristine Choeng-Mon beach in the north east of Thai island Koh Samui, this spa resort offers a secluded hideaway for beach lovers. Even so, it is just a few minutes to the nearby fisherman's village of Bo Phut and the bars and boutiques of the Chaweng Beach are also situated a convenient distance away for a shopping trip or the last drink of the night. The 69 facilities of the luxury villas are a mixture of traditional Thai architecture and modern design. Gleaming white walls, upholstery, linen covers and fabric lengths effectively contrast with the sparingly used dark teak woods of the flooring and furniture. Guests can choose from villas with one or two bedrooms. 53 bungalows open out onto a private garden with its own mini swimming pool. And you can even keep an eye out for shooting stars whilst showering, as the bathrooms are also partly under open, tropical skies. To perfect the indulgence guests can be spoiled in the Mandara Spa under the rules of the Asian art of relaxation. If desired you can even have your massage on a floating deck by the main pool. In appropriate style next to blooming lotus flowers.

Relaxen unter einem Tempelbaum: Am bisher noch weitgehend unberührten Choeng-Mon-Beach im Nordosten der thailändischen Insel Koh Samui bietet dieses Spa-Resort für Strandliebhaber ein verschwiegenes Hideaway. Trotzdem sind es bis zum nahegelegenen Fischerdorf Bo Phut nur ein paar Minuten, und auch die Bars und Boutiquen des Chaweng Beach liegen noch in erreichbarer Nähe für einen Shopping-Ausflug oder den abendlichen Absacker. Die 69 Einrichtungen der Luxusvillen sind eine Mischung aus traditioneller Thai-Architektur und modernem Design. Leuchtend weiße Wände, Polster, Leinenbezüge und Stoffbahnen kontrastieren wirkungsvoll mit sparsam eingesetzten dunklen Teakhölzern der Fußböden und Möbel. Zur Auswahl stehen Villen mit einem oder zwei Schlafzimmern. 53 Bungalows öffnen sich zu einem privaten Garten mit einem eigenen Mini-Schwimmbad. Sogar beim Duschen kann man hier nach Sternschnuppen Ausschau halten, denn auch die Badezimmer befinden sich teilweise unter freiem Tropenhimmel. Um die Erholung vollkommen zu machen, können sich die Gäste im Mandara-Spa nach allen Regeln der asiatischen Entspannungskunst verwöhnen lassen. Die Massagen werden auf Wunsch auch auf schwimmenden Decks am Hauptpool verabreicht. Stilgerecht neben blühenden Lotosblumen.

01 | Cooling down on an evening: you can jump straight from the couch into your very own pool.

Abkühlung am Abend: Von der Couch geht es direkt in den eigenen Pool.

02 | Saltwater can be rinsed from the skin in the open air bathtub.

In der Badewanne kann man sich openair das Salzwasser von der Haut spülen.

03 | The interior is characterized by light colors and clear lines.

Das Interieur ist geprägt von hellen Farben und klaren Linien.

04 | The roof is inspired by Thai temple architecture, the highlight by the pool is a sheltered day bed.

Das Dach ist von der thailändischen Tempelarchitektur inspiriert, das Highlight am Pool ein überdachtes Tagesbett.

04

voyages dunk island | tropical north queensland . australia
DESIGN: Justin Long

Visitors to the Great Barrier Reef only have one thing on their minds: diving—under the surface of the water and away from everyday stress. Voyages Dunk Island is the perfect place for both of these. The approximately 2,471 acres large island is located around three kilometers from the coast of Queensland in the north of Australia. Most of the tropical rainforest, which covers it, is protected under nature conservation laws. Located right in the middle of this landscape, the hotel is an oasis in itself. The 160 rooms and suites can be found either in the fairytale-like forest or right on the palm tree lined beach. But their decoration—like life on the island—is determined by the sea. The turtles, with which the guests can enter into a snorkeling competition, can also be found again in traditional drawings on the walls. Bed linen and upholstery shimmer in all facets of the ocean from turquoise to deep sea blue. Classic wicker furniture and light tiles form the subdued basis. Large windows frame the view of the exotic island world. If you want to give swimming a miss for once, it's also possible to hire mountain bikes, go riding, play golf or be spoiled in the six bars and cafés of the resort.

Wer das Great Barrier Reef besucht, hat vor allem eins im Sinn: Abtauchen – unter die Wasseroberfläche und vom Alltagsstress. Für beides ist Voyages Dunk Island der perfekte Ort. Die etwa 1000 Hektar große Insel liegt rund vier Kilometer vor der Küste von Queensland im Norden Australiens. Der tropische Regenwald, der sie bedeckt, steht in weiten Teilen unter Naturschutz. Inmitten dieser Landschaft ist das Hotel eine Oase für sich. Die 160 Zimmer und Suiten liegen entweder im märchenhaften Wald oder direkt am mit Palmen gesäumten Strand. Ihre Einrichtung wird aber – wie das gesamte Leben auf der Insel – vom Meer bestimmt. Die Schildkröten, mit denen die Gäste tagsüber um die Wette schnorcheln, finden sich auch auf traditionellen Zeichnungen an den Wänden wieder. Bettwäsche und Polstermöbel schimmern in allen Fassetten des Ozeans von Türkis bis Tiefseeblau. Klassische Korbmöbel und helle Fliesen bilden die dezente Basis. Große Fenster rahmen den Blick auf die exotische Inselwelt ein. Wer einmal nicht schwimmen möchte, kann sich Mountainbikes mieten, Reitausflüge machen, golfen oder sich in den sechs Bars und Cafés des Resorts verwöhnen lassen.

01 | The first inhabitants called Dunk Island "Coonanglebah"—the Island of Peace and Plenty.

„Coonanglebah" – Insel des Friedens und des Überflusses, so nannten die Ureinwohner Dunk Island.

02

03

02 | Whilst sunbathing on the private terrace you'll have the feeling that the beach is yours alone.

Wer sich auf der privaten Terrasse sonnt, hat den Eindruck, dass auch der Strand nur ihm allein gehört.

03 | On request an exclusive barbecue can be arranged in front of the rooms located on the beach.

Auf Wunsch wird vor den am Strand gelegenen Zimmern ein exklusives Barbecue arrangiert.

04 | All rooms have balconies or terraces.

Alle Zimmer verfügen über Balkone oder Terrassen.

05 | 06 The biggest disturbance of serenity in the spa will be by the snorting of surfacing sea turtles.

Die Ruhe im Spa wird höchstens durch das Prusten auftauchender Meeresschildkröten gestört.

01 | Hotel guests can anchor their private boats in the protected harbor.
Im geschützten Hafen können Hotelgäste mit ihren Privatbooten ankern.

couran cove island resort | south stradbroke island . australia
DESIGN: Daryl Jackson

Swimming, sailing, diving, fishing or surfing are just some of the kinds of water sports that the resort has to offer. Plus there are countless activities on land, from guided rambles to climbing tours. And alone the exploration of the 14 miles long beach offers enough variety. And as there are enough impressions to digest during the day, the rooms have more of a tasteful and demure design. Classic shapes and colors never distract from the views and convey tranquility. The azure blue sky and steel blue sea are reflected in panes of the panoramic window. All rooms and suites of this impressive facility can be found right next to the water. This is not just the ideal accommodation for couples; large families also have plenty of space in the villas, which have up to four bedrooms. You also have the choice of going to one of the hotel's four restaurants to eat, or to cook yourself as the villas are equipped with all the amenities of a modern house. With so much space and variety it is only logical that brides and grooms travel here with their entire wedding parties.

Schwimmen, Segeln, Tauchen, Fischen oder Surfen sind nur ein Teil der Wassersportarten, die das Resort im Angebot hat. Hinzu kommen zahlreiche Aktivitäten auf dem Land, von geführten Wanderungen bis hin zu Klettertouren. Dabei bietet allein die Erkundung des 22 Kilometer langen Strandes genug Abwechslung. Wohl weil es tagsüber genügend Eindrücke zu verarbeiten gibt, sind die Zimmer betont geschmackvoll und zurückhaltend gestaltet. Klassische Formen und Farben lassen den Blick nirgends anecken und vermitteln Ruhe. In den Scheiben der Panoramafenster spiegeln sich der azurblaue Himmel und das stahlblaue Meer. Sämtliche Zimmer und Suiten der beeindruckenden Anlage liegen unmittelbar am Wasser. Hier finden nicht nur Paare die ideale Unterkunft, auch Großfamilien haben in den bis zu vier Schlafzimmer umfassenden Villen jede Menge Platz. Sie können auch wählen, ob Sie zum Essen in eines von vier hoteleigenen Restaurants gehen oder lieber selbst kochen. Schließlich sind die Villen mit allen Annehmlichkeiten eines modernen Hauses ausgestattet. Bei so viel Platz und Vielfalt ist es nur logisch, dass auch Hochzeitspaare mit der kompletten Hochzeitsgesellschaft anreisen.

02 | The free standing lodges are equipped with their own kitchens.
   Die frei stehenden Lodges sind mit einer eigenen Küche ausgestattet.

03 | Some of the rooms and suites can only be reached by jetties.
   Einige der Zimmer und Suiten sind nur über Stege zu erreichen.

04 | Guests can observe the goings on in the lagoon whilst enjoying breakfast on the terrace.
Beim Frühstück auf der Terrasse kann der Gast das Treiben in der Lagune beobachten.

05 | The standard rooms are also situated right on the water.
Auch die Standard-Zimmer liegen direkt am Wasser.

01 | Pool or Pacific? The resort's four villas offer both options.
Pool oder Pazifik? Die vier Villen des Resorts bieten beide Optionen.

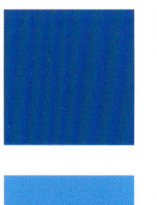

eagles nest kohanga ekara | bay of islands . new zealand
DESIGN: Sandra and Daniel Biskind

A journey to the other end of the world: on a small group of islands off the coast of New Zealand Eagles Nest Kohanga Ekara huddles against the ridge of a group of hills. Surrounded by subtropical nature, with the South Pacific with private beaches right on the doorstep, the setting with its elegant minimalistic design is imbedded into the original landscape. On the 15 acre premises, four luxury villas offer all amenities, including designer kitchen and pool, as well as personal and chef upon request. Each of the villas has a specific ambience, through the exquisite antique furniture as well as modern objets d'art. In the nearby surroundings numerous hiking trails are waiting to be discovered—or you can enjoy the impressive sunset and the exuberant playfulness of the dolphins and whales on the beach. As well as wellness treatments—the therapists come right into the villas—numerous leisure time activities are on offer. Top of the list are fishing and diving, but also water skiing, kayaking or parasailing are on offer. An exquisite gourmet cuisine with a varied choice of products from New Zealand—lots of the tasty ingredients come from the hotel's own gardens—provides sustenance. In addition, once a week the members of the local Nga Puhi tribe visit Eagles Nest Kohanga Ekara, to tell the stories of their ancestors through song and dance.

Eine Reise ans andere Ende der Welt: Auf einer kleinen Inselgruppe vor Neuseeland schmiegt sich das Eagles Nest Kohanga Ekara an den Kamm einer Hügelkette. Umgeben von subtropischer Natur, den Südpazifik mit Privatstränden direkt vor der Haustür, bettet sich die Anlage mit ihrem elegant-minimalistischen Design in die ursprüngliche Landschaft ein. Auf dem 30 Hektar großen Anwesen bieten vier Luxusvillen alle Annehmlichkeiten, zu denen unter anderem Designerküche und Pool sowie auf Wunsch ein eigener Butler und Koch zählen. Jede der Villen besitzt ein spezifisches Ambiente, etwa durch erlesene antike Möbel oder aber durch moderne Kunstobjekte. In der Umgebung laden zahlreiche Wanderwege zur Erkundung ein – oder aber man genießt am Strand den imposanten Sonnenuntergang und das ausgelassene Spiel der Delfine und Wale. Neben Wellness-Anwendungen – die Therapeuten kommen direkt in die Villen – bieten sich zahlreiche Freizeitaktivitäten an. Allen voran Großfischfang und Tauchen, aber auch Wasserski, Kajakfahren oder Fallschirmsegeln. Eine erlesene Feinschmeckerküche mit einer vielfältigen Auswahl neuseeländischer Produkte – viele der geschmackvollen Zutaten stammen aus den hauseigenen Gartenanlagen – sorgt für das leibliche Wohl. Darüber hinaus sind einmal pro Woche Angehörige des lokalen Nga Puhi-Stammes in Eagles Nest Kohanga Ekara zu Gast, die mit Tänzen und Gesängen in die Geschichte ihrer Vorfahren eintauchen.

02 | The feel-good concept is extended deep into the night: guests sleep in designer bed linen.
Wohlfühl-Konzept bis hin zur Nachtruhe: Die Gäste schlafen in Designerbettwäsche.

03 | Every suite has a designer kitchen—which even comes with its own chef if desired.
Jede Suite verfügt über eine Designerküche – auf Wunsch sogar mit eigenem Koch.

04 | The lavish living area with fireplace in the "First Light Temple" villa.
   Der großzügige Wohnbereich mit Kamin in der Villa „First Light Temple".

05 | Light-flooded suite with panoramic view over the landscape and the ocean.
   Lichtdurchflutete Suite mit Panoramablick auf die Landschaft und das Meer.

01 | The palm-covered roofs huddle closely against the tropical green hillside.
Die palmengedeckten Dächer schmiegen sich eng an den tropisch grünen Hang.

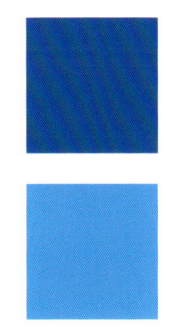

bora bora nui resort & spa | bora bora . french polynesia
DESIGN: Pierre Lacombe, Lulu Wane

Guests embark on the last leg of their journey by motor yacht, which adds to that luxury feeling. After 10 minutes the boat reaches the landing stage of the resort. It lies in a little bay on the cusp of one of the many smaller islands of Bora Bora: a setting with stilt houses over the water, which stretch out along the pure white beach. Some of the 120 villa suites are hidden in a lagoon; the rest can be found in the hills at the rear of the resort. A meandering line of wooden landing stages connects the individual bungalows. With their traditional design of faded wood and reed roofs they help to create that South Pacific feeling. The overwater bungalows with glass floors are an attraction in themselves. Western comforts like refrigerators are omitted instead, you will be indulged with treats like marble bathrooms and mahogany four poster beds. The terrace with a platform for swimming means you can jump straight into the sea. And the resort has a lot to offer just-married couples, including a joint spa treatment in your own room.

Das letzte Stück der Anreise nehmen die Gäste mit einer Motoryacht, die es versteht, ein Gefühl von Luxus zu verströmen. Nach zehn Minuten erreicht das Schiff den Landesteg des Resorts. Dieses liegt in einer kleinen Bucht am Zipfel einer der vielen Nebeninseln von Bora Bora: eine Anlage mit Pfahlbauten über Wasser, die sich entlang des hellweißen Strandes erstreckt. Ein Teil der 120 Villensuiten versteckt sich in einer Lagune, ein anderer in den Hügeln im Rücken des Resorts. Ein sich schlängelndes Band aus Holzstegen verbindet die einzelnen Bungalows. Mit ihrer traditionellen Bauweise aus verblichenem Holz und innen offenen Dächern aus Reet gelingt es ihnen, ursprüngliches Südseefeeling anzustimmen. Eine Attraktion für sich stellen die Überwasserbungalows dar, die mit einem Glasboden aufwarten. Die Ausstattung verzichtet auf westliche Errungenschaften wie einen Kühlschrank. Dafür verwöhnen Bäder aus Marmor und Himmelbetten aus Mahagoni. Die Terrasse mit einer Plattform zum Baden erlaubt zudem ohne Umwege den Sprung in die Fluten. Denen, die sich frisch getraut haben, bietet das Resort einige spezielle Angebote. Zu ihnen gehört eine gemeinsame Spa-Behandlung in den eigenen Räumen.

02

02 | When there's a storm in the air, the South Pacific looks more like a painting than ever.

Bei Gewitterstimmung wirkt die Südsee erst recht wie ein Gemälde.

03 | White sun shades and loungers surround the big pool.

Weiße Sonnenschirme und Liegestühle umrahmen den ausladenden Pool.

04 | The restaurant is sheltered by a high bamboo roof.

Das Restaurant wird von einem hohen Bambusdach beschirmt.

01 | The rooms with a noble Asia design open up to gorgeous views.
Die Zimmer im edlen Asia-Design eröffnen traumhafte Aussichten.

the setai | miami south beach . florida

DESIGN: Jaya Pratomo Ibrahim from Jaya & Associates; Jean Michel Gathy from Denniston International

Miami South Beach—has long since been a synonym for summer, sun, beach and art deco. But with the opening of The Setai in 2005 the American hotel business is also experiencing what Asian hospitality means. The building on Collins Avenue was originally the Dempsey Vanderbilt Hotel in the 1930's. With a group of investors the founder of Amanresort, Adrian Zecha, transformed the building on the seemingly never-ending beach of Miami. It is enthroned amongst tropical palm gardens with azure blue pools and is connected to the white sandy beach on the Atlantic. In The Setai Zecha has managed to revive long-since forgotten American splendor and glamour and merge it with echoes of the ornate art deco era of Shanghai. The lobby is a dream of teak and bronze, in the 75 rooms and 50 suites soft silhouettes, light fabrics and granite bathrooms with Acqua di Parma accessories create a noble understatement and the views are purely breathtaking. Zechas' appreciation for highly personal service and complete privacy is also apparent in the spa, which has a touch of the Far East, with magnificent spa suites and in the restaurant with its trans-ethnic cuisine.

Miami South Beach – das ist schon lange ein Synonym für Sommer, Sonne, Strand und Art déco. Mit Eröffnung des The Setai im Jahr 2005 erlebt die amerikanische Hotellerie aber auch, was asiatische Gastfreundschaft bedeutet. Das Gebäude an der Collins Avenue war in den 1930ern ursprünglich das Dempsey Vanderbilt Hotel. Dahinter hat der Amanresort Gründer Adrian Zecha mit einer Investorengruppe das höchste Gebäude am endlos erscheinenden Strand von Miami erbauen lassen. Es thront inmitten tropischer Palmengärten mit azurblauen Pools und ist direkt mit dem weißen Sandstrand am Atlantik verbunden. Zecha lässt im The Setai längst vergessen geglaubten amerikanischen Glanz und Glamour wieder aufleben und verbindet ihn mit Anklängen an die kunstvolle Art déco-Ära von Shanghai. Die Lobby ist ein Traum aus Teak und Bronze. In den 75 Zimmern und 50 Suiten sorgen weiche Silhouetten, helle Stoffe und Granitbäder mit Accessoires von Acqua di Parma für edles Understatement, und die Aussichten sind schlicht atemberaubend. Zechas Sinn für höchstpersönlichen Service und Privatsphäre pur zeigt sich auch im fernöstlich angehauchten Spa mit herrlichen Spa-Suiten und im Restaurant mit trans-ethnischer Küche.

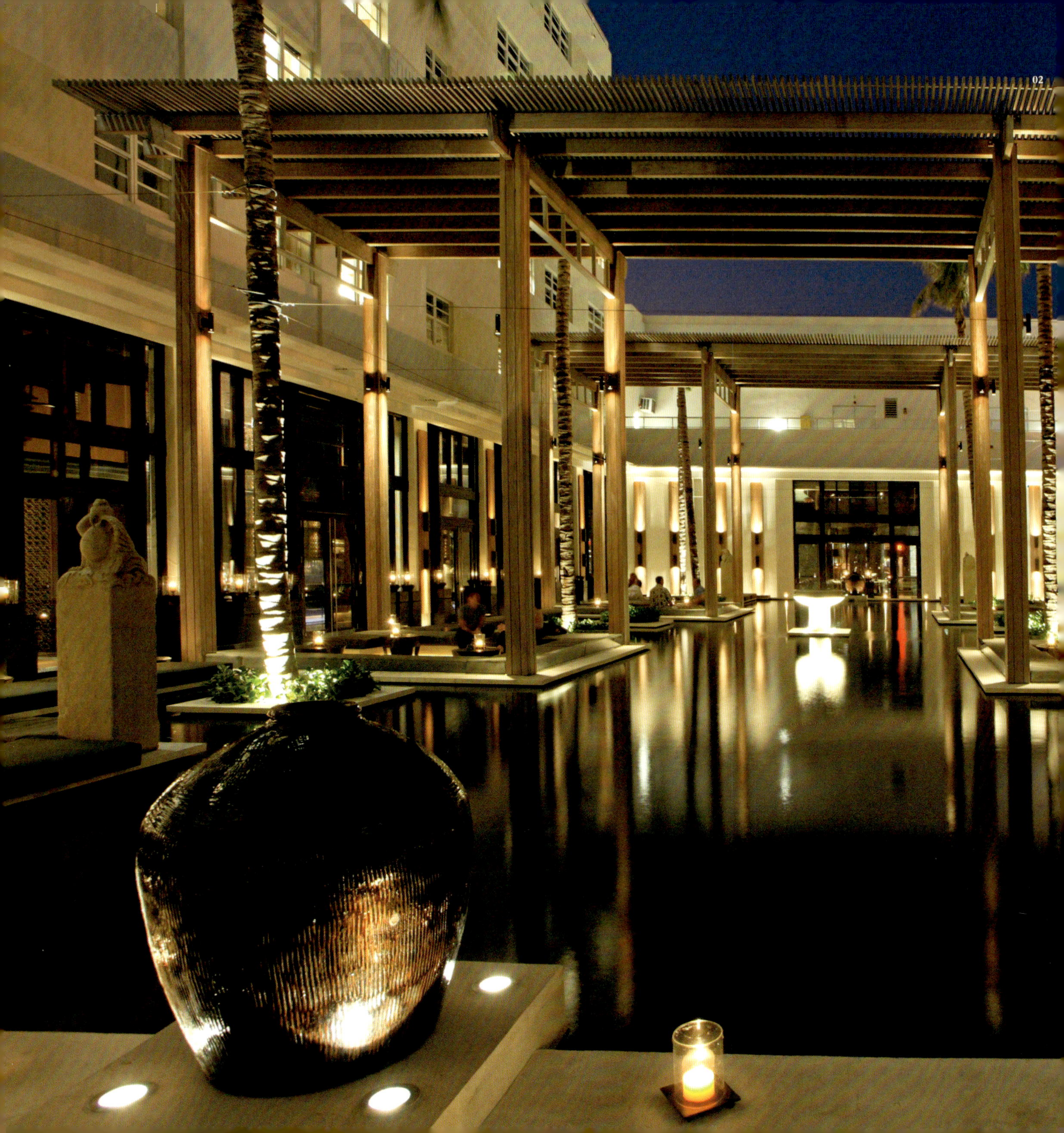
02

02 | At night the inner courtyard transforms into a lounge with a symphony of lights.

Nachts verwandelt sich der Innenhof in eine Lounge-Sinfonie der Lichter.

03 | The apartments of the high-rise building, which can also be rented as hotel rooms, show the glittering metropolis at its best, especially just before sunset.

Die auch als Hotelzimmer mietbaren Appartements des angeschlossenen Hochhauses zeigen die Glitzermetropole zur blauen Stunde besonders schön.

04 | Three pools and countless palm trees help to make the The Setai such an idyllic city and beach oasis.

Drei Pools und ungezählte Palmen machen The Setai zur idyllischen Stadt- und Strandoase.

01 | The blue of the pool is a gentle contrast to that of the Caribbean.
Sanft kontrastiert das Blau des Pools mit dem der Karibik.

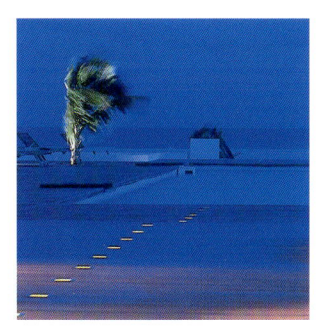

the beach house barbuda | barbuda . british west indies
DESIGN: OBM International, Linda Blair & Associates

It's all in the name here. The hotel, after an elaborate renovation, is now presented in a luxury design. The modern 20 suites, full of cool colors and airy fabrics, have exclusive bathrooms and private terraces with ocean views. A composition of white walls and dark teak wood characterizes the ambience of the suites. The centerpiece of the hotel is the Club House, where open architecture makes use of the cooling trade winds. The hotel restaurant with a bar offers Italian/Caribbean fusion cuisine, which upon request can also be served anywhere on the property. The private hotel beach stretches directly in front of the grounds, where countless seashells are immersed in a colored kaleidoscope. The facets range from lily, white to baby pink. Spectacular views can be enjoyed from the bird protection reserve, where thousands of imposing Frigate birds with wingspans of up to seven feet can be observed. Barbuda, located around 25 miles from its well-known sister island Antigua, is surrounded by coral reefs, which are just as appealing for divers as the vast numbers of shipwrecks.

Hier ist der Name Programm. Direkt am feinsandigen Strand der Karibikinsel Barbuda liegt das Hotel, das sich nach aufwändiger Renovierung in luxuriösem Design präsentiert. Die modernen, in kühlen Farben und luftigen Stoffen gehaltenen 20 Suiten verfügen über exklusive Bäder und private Terrassen mit Meeresblick. Eine Komposition aus weißen Wänden und dunklem Teakholz prägt das Ambiente der Suiten. Herzstück der Hotelanlage ist das Club House, dessen offene Architektur die kühlenden Passatwinde nutzt. Das Hotelrestaurant mit Bar offeriert italienisch karibische Spezialitäten, die auf Wunsch auch auf dem gesamten Hotelgelände serviert werden. Direkt vor der Anlage erstreckt sich der private Hotelstrand, den unzählige Muschelschalen in ein farbiges Kaleidoskop tauchen. Die Fassetten reichen von blütenweiß bis zartrosa. Spektakuläre Aussichten bieten sich im Vogelschutzreservat, in dem Tausende der imposanten Fregattvögel mit Spannweiten bis zu zwei Metern beobachtet werden können. Barbuda, rund 40 Kilometer von der bekannten Schwesterinsel Antigua entfernt, ist ringsherum von Korallenriffen gesäumt, die ebenso zu einem Tauchgang einladen wie die zahllosen Schiffwracks.

02 | The color white characterizes the ambience of the rooms.
Die Farbe Weiß prägt das Ambiente der Zimmer.

03 | At evening the lights gently sparkle on the pool.
Sanft strahlen am Abend die Lichter auf den Pool.

04 | A splendid place to relax is under the white awnings.
Unter weißen Sonnensegeln lässt es sich trefflich relaxen.

04

eden rock | st. barthélemy . caribbean
DESIGN: Jane Matthews, David Matthews

As the name already suggests: Eden Rock is paradise on a rock. To be precise: a small rugged peninsula, which rises out of the turquoise blue Atlantic Ocean in the French Caribbean. In the 50's a private citizen chose this hamlet in the bay of St. Jean as his beach house. In the mid-90's an English couple Jane and David Matthews bought the exposed situated tropical premises and converted it into a grand-scale vacation home. The hotel business began with a beach bar and expanded from there. Pamela Parker, Jane's sister, supported her relatives with her great taste in the construction of an exquisite beach resort, which merges Caribbean flair with the classic ambience of an English country residence. At twilight, when lamps and candles are burning in the suites and rooms, the Eden Rock sparkles like a gemstone in the ocean. Its highlight is the Diamond Suite Loft situated on a hill. It doesn't just have its own infinity pool, but also its own beach cottage by the sea. Every room has an individual touch and is decorated in different colors. Many have a canopy bed.

Der Name deutet es bereits an: Das Eden Rock ist ein Paradies auf einem Felsen. Genauer gesagt: auf einer kleinen felsigen Halbinsel, die sich in der französischen Karibik aus dem dem türkisblauen Atlantischen Ozean erhebt. Ein Privatmann suchte sich bereits in den 50er-Jahren diesen Flecken in der Bucht von St. Jean für sein Stranddomizil aus. Mitte der 90er-Jahre kaufte sich das englische Ehepaar Jane und David Matthews das exponiert gelegene Tropenanwesen und baute es zu einem großzügigen Ferienhaus um. Der Hotelbetrieb begann mit einer Beach-Bar und weitete sich aus. Pamela Parker, die Schwester von Jane, unterstützte ihre Verwandten mit viel Geschmack bei der Errichtung eines exquisiten Strandresorts, das karibisches Flair mit dem klassischen Ambiente eines englischen Landsitzes verbindet. In der Dämmerung, wenn in den Suiten und Zimmern die Lampen und Kerzen angezündet sind, funkelt das Eden Rock wie ein Edelstein im Ozean. Sein Höhepunkt ist die auf einem Hügel gelegene Diamont Suite Loft. Sie verfügt nicht nur über einen eigenen Infinitypool, sondern auch über ein eigenes Beach Cottage am Meer. Jedes Zimmer hat seine eigene individuelle Note und ist in anderen Farben dekoriert. Viele haben ein Himmelbett.

01 | Wood is the defining material in this beach resort built into a rock.

Holz ist der bestimmende Werkstoff des in den Felsen gebauten Starndresorts.

02

02 | A box seat, with ship-like railing.

Ein Logenplatz, dessen Reling an ein Schiff erinnert.

03 | Art and cushions set colorful trends in the bedroom.

Kunst und Kissen setzen knallige Akzente im Schlafzimmer.

04 | The ocean is also visible from the living room.

Auch vom Wohnzimmer aus ist das Meer im Blickfeld.

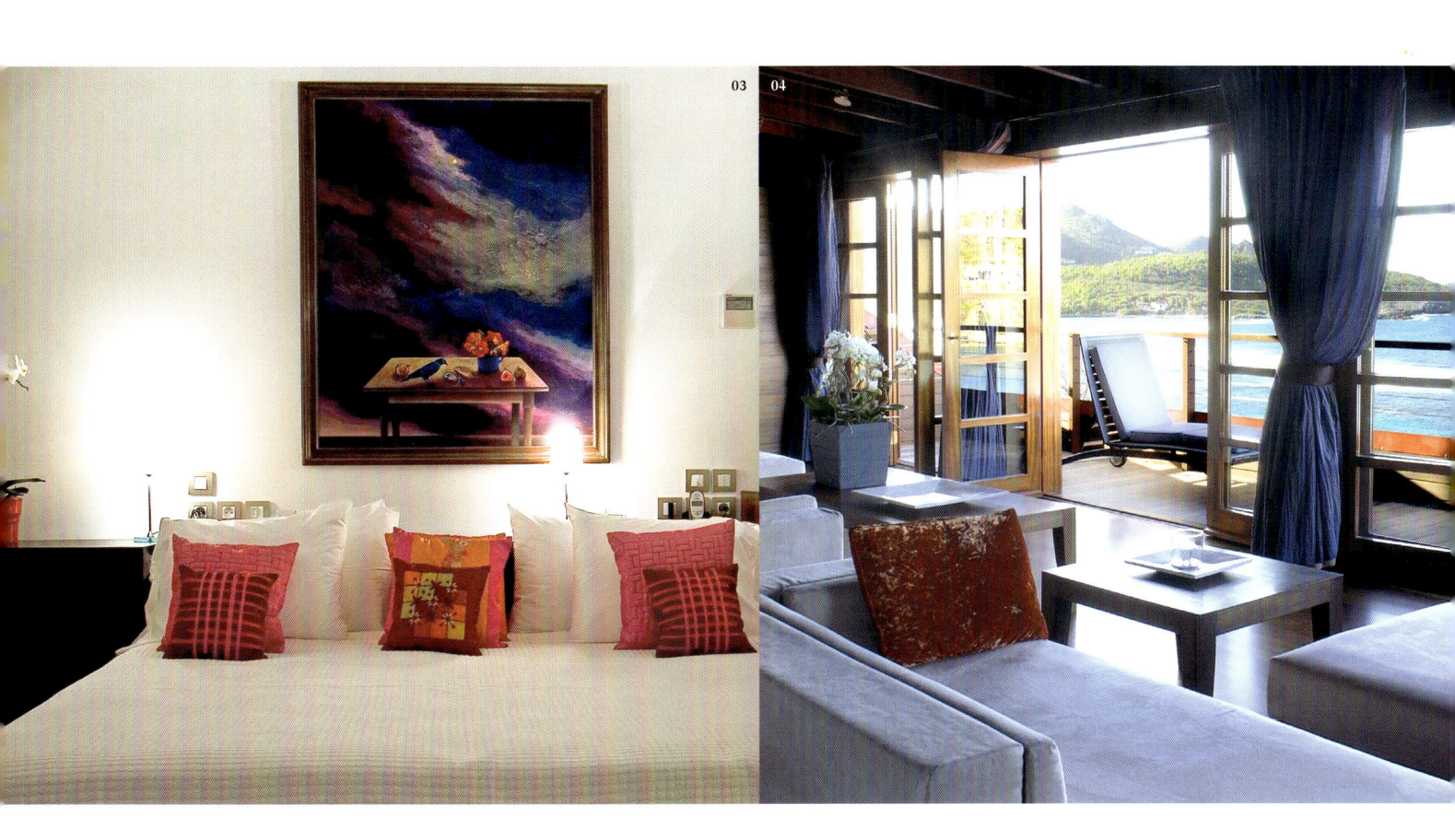

05 | When night falls Eden Rock is illuminated far beyond the beach of St. Jean.

Nachts leuchtet das Eden Rock weit über den Strand von St. Jean.

06 | Each of the rooms has its own style, here the walls are designed with a large surface using a spatula technique.

Jedes der Zimmer hat einen eigenen Stil. Hier sind die Wände mit größflächiger Spachteltechnik gestaltet.

las alamandas | puerto vallarta . mexico
DESIGN: Gabriel Nunez, Isabel Goldsmith

Every color of the rainbow can be found in this lovingly designed house. Guests don't have to look for very long to find the inspiration for the decoration. The hidden resort, a two-hour drive south of Puerto Vallarta, is surrounded by turquoise colored sea, bright blue sky, palm trees and colored blooms. Owner Isabel Goldsmith has fulfilled a childhood dream with this hotel. Her personal style and her sense of humor not only characterize the interior design, but also the entire architecture. And she places great value upon the integration of local handicraft tradition. Also in terms of service Las Alamandas focuses less on high tech and more on individuality. So, guests will be searching to no avail for plasma televisions in their suites. Instead they will find a daily newspaper in front of the door every morning. The 15 suites are accommodated in typical Mexican country houses. All have their own terrace with views over the enchanting tropical garden or the glistening sea with its secluded, seemingly neverending sandy beach. The three honeymoon suites are especially spacious and each one has a special element. For example Casa San Antonio boasts it own outdoor whirlpool. If you'd really like to indulge yourself, you can order Mexican finger food from the hotel restaurants directly to this pool.

Alle Farben des Regenbogens finden sich in diesem liebevoll gestalteten Haus. Dabei muss der Gast nicht lange suchen, um die Inspiration für die Einrichtung zu finden. Das versteckt liegende Resort, zwei Autostunden südlich von Puerto Vallarta, ist von türkisfarbenem Meer, strahlend blauem Himmel, Palmen und farbigen Blüten umgeben. Besitzerin Isabel Goldsmith hat sich mit diesem Hotel einen Kindheitstraum erfüllt. Ihr persönlicher Stil und ihr Sinn für Humor prägen nicht nur die Inneneinrichtung, sondern die gesamte Architektur. Dabei legte sie besonderen Wert auf die Einbindung lokaler Handwerkstradition. Auch in punkto Service setzt das Las Alamandas weniger auf Hightech als auf Individualität. So sucht der Gast vergebens nach einem Flachbildfernseher in seiner Suite. Dafür findet er jeden Morgen eine Tageszeitung vor der Tür. Die 15 Suiten sind in typisch mexikanischen Landhäusern untergebracht. Alle haben eine eigene Terrasse mit Blick in den verwunschenen tropischen Garten oder das glitzernde Meer mit seinem einsamen, unendlich erscheinenden Sandstrand. Die drei Honeymoon-Suiten sind sehr geräumig und haben jeweils ein besonderes Element. Zur Casa San Antonio gehört beispielsweise ein eigener Outdoor-Whirlpool. Wer sich ganz besonders verwöhnen lassen möchte, kann mexikanisches Fingerfood des hauseigenen Restaurants direkt zu diesem Pool bestellen.

01 | Guests can admire the most beautiful view from the private rooftop terraces of Casa San Antonio and Casa San Miguel.

Den schönsten Blick genießt der Gast von den privaten Dachterrassen der Casa San Antonio und der Casa San Miguel.

02 | The suites are reminiscent of a luxury version of Villa Kunterbunt—they represent the childhood dreams of the proprietor.

Die Suiten erinnern an eine Luxusversion der Villa Kunterbunt – sie stehen für die Kindheitsträume der Eigentümerin.

03 | Contrary to anonymous hotel chains, the furnishing with traditional elements, is supposed to consciously remind the guests of which country they are in.

Die Einrichtung mit traditionellen Elementen soll, im Gegensatz zu anonymen Hotelketten, ganz bewusst daran erinnern, in welchem Land sich der Gast befindet.

04 | Romantic alcoves invite guests to explore the entire hotel grounds.

Romantische Nischen laden auf dem gesamten Hotelgelände zum Entdecken ein.

04

hotel azúcar | veracruz . mexico
DESIGN: Carlos Couturier, Elias Adam and Jose Robredo

As white as sugar—is how one could describe the outer walls of the 20 bungalows, which form the retreat of the Hotel Azúcar (Spanish for sugar). The holiday resort is located on the Gulf of Mexico, imbedded in a forest of palm trees. In the center of the setting, which is characterized by light colored tones, is the pool. The arrangement of the flat houses and calm zones around the waters convey a lounge and club atmosphere. The thatched palapas can be reached by well-laid paths. As the sun shines almost every day, the roofs only serve as protection from the heat. Like the outer walls, the interior of the bungalows is also dominated by colored tones. Only the scarce furniture acts as a contrast to this. Also the hotel's library, which can be found in the fresh air, more resembles a lounge than a study room. Guests enjoy spending time here, browsing or reading a book. If you're more adventurous, you can go on a bike ride to the nearby vanilla plantations. Those searching for relaxation can regenerate in the meditation room or simply relax your mind during a walk along the mile long beaches.

Weiß wie Zucker – so könnte man die Außenwände der 20 Bungalows beschreiben, die die Anlage des Hotels Azúcar (spanisch für Zucker) bilden. Das Ferienresort befindet sich direkt am Golf von Mexiko, eingebettet in einen Palmenwald. Im Zentrum der von hellen Farbtönen geprägten Anlage befindet sich ein Pool. Die Anordnung der flachen Häuser und Ruhezonen um das Gewässer herum vermittelt Lounge- und Club-Atmosphäre. Zu erreichen sind die mit Strohdächern bedeckten Gebäude über schön angelegte Pfade. Da nahezu jeden Tag die Sonne scheint, dienen die Dächer nur zum Schutz vor der Hitze. Wie die Außenwände, so wird auch das Interieur der Bungalows von weißen Farbtönen dominiert. Den Kontrast hierzu bildet einzig die sparsame Holzmöblierung. Auch die hoteleigene Bibliothek, die sich an der frischen Luft befindet, ähnelt eher einer Lounge als einem Studierzimmer. Gerne verweilen die Gäste hier und stöbern oder lesen ein Buch. Wer unternehmungslustig ist, hat die Möglichkeit mit dem Fahrrad die nicht weit entfernten Vanille-Plantagen zu besuchen. Entspannungs-Suchende können sich außerdem im Meditationsraum erholen oder bei einem Spaziergang an den kilometerlangen Stränden einfach die Seele baumeln lassen.

01 | Still life on the beach: sleek changing cubicles of the Hotel Azúcar.

Stillife am Strand: schlichte Umkleidekabinen des Hotels Azúcar.

02 | One bed, one chair, white walls: sheer purism in the bedrooms.
Ein Bett, ein Stuhl, weiße Wände: Purismus pur in den Schlafzimmern.

03 | Lounge atmosphere: the surroundings of the hotel pool.
Lounge-Atmosphäre: die Umgebung des Hotel-Pools.

04 | The bungalows are built between palm trees, right by the water.
Die Bungalows sind zwischen Palmen und direkt am Wasser erbaut.

05 | A place of calm and relaxation: the library.
Ort der Ruhe und Entspannung: die Bibliothek.

biblioteca

01 | Guests also have the opportunity to linger on the beach at night, where they can enjoy the splashing of the ocean over a cocktail.

Auch nachts haben die Gäste die Möglichkeit, sich am Strand aufzuhalten und bei einem Cocktail das Rauschen des Meeres zu genießen.

esencia | riviera maya . mexico
DESIGN: Prohotel International, Alfonso Nuñez

Light and air are the central elements of a perfect holiday. Both are in abundance in this hotel and the entire design concept seems to be in coordination with this. Countless large sun terraces are grouped around the three-storey main building, the former villa of an Italian noble family. Open corridors with bricked arches and large entrance areas blur the boundaries between inside and out. White is the dominating color in the nine rooms and the ten garden suites, so the decoration comes across as demurely elegant, without seeming minimalistically cool. Providing the Mexican touch are dark, almost black wooden furniture and accessories as well as specifically placed colored elements, like bed spreads or tropical fruits, which guests can pick themselves during a stroll around the 50 acres of grounds. If you prefer to spend a beach holiday with friends or with the whole family, Esencia offers several villas with a private pool. It's only a few steps away to the pristine seashore. The beach, which is over two miles long, is also the starting point for leisure activities; everything from fishing and diving trips to sailing boat tours. On the other hand, the ideal place for lazy days is the stylish hammocks tucked away throughout the grounds.

Licht und Luft sind die zentralen Elemente eines perfekten Urlaubs. Beides gibt es in diesem Hotel im Überfluss. Schließlich scheint das gesamte Designkonzept darauf abgestimmt. Zahlreiche große Sonnenterrassen gruppieren sich um das drei Stockwerke hohe Hauptgebäude, die ehemalige Villa einer italienischen Adelsfamilie. Offene Gänge mit gemauerten Bögen und großzügige Eingangsbereiche lassen die Grenzen zwischen innen und außen verschwimmen. Weiß ist die dominierende Farbe in den neun Zimmern und den zehn Garten-Suiten. So wirkt die Ausstattung zurückhaltend elegant, ohne minimalistisch kühl zu erscheinen. Für mexikanische Akzente sorgen dunkle, fast schwarze Holzmöbel und Accessoires sowie gezielt platzierte farbige Elemente wie Tagesdecken oder tropische Früchte. Diese kann man bei einem Spaziergang über das 20 Hektar große Gelände auch selbst pflücken. Wer den Strandurlaub am liebsten mit Freunden oder der ganzen Familie verbringt, dem bietet das Esencia eigene Villen mit privatem Pool. Zum unberührten Meeresufer sind es nur wenige Schritte. Der über drei Kilometer lange Strand ist auch Ausgangspunkt für Freizeitaktivitäten von Angel- und Tauchausflügen bis hin zu Touren mit dem Segelschiff. Der ideale Ort für faule Tage sind dagegen die stilechten Hängematten, die sich versteckt auf dem Gelände befinden.

02 | This hotel is especially proud of its cuisine; the guests can even catch their own fresh fish.

Besonders stolz ist man im Hotel auf die Küche. Frischen Fisch können die Gäste auch selbst angeln.

03 | Guests can enjoy the view of the ocean from each of the nine rooms in the main house, but also the suites in the villas offer beautiful vistas of tropical vegetation and the sea.

Von jedem der neun Zimmer im Haupthaus kann der Gast den Ausblick auf den Ozean genießen. Doch auch die Suiten in den Villen bieten neben eigenem Planschpool schöne Aussichten auf tropische Vegetation und Meer.

esencia | 149

04 | The house which opened in 2006 shows a local attachment with its architecture and a world class level with its service.

Das 2006 eröffnete Haus zeigt lokale Verbundenheit mit seiner Architektur und Weltniveau mit seinem Service.

05 | Two pools border the fine sandy, white beach.
Zwei Pools grenzen direkt an den feinsandig, weißen Strand.

esencia | 151

casa de los sueños resort and spa | isla mujeres . mexico
DESIGN: Alma Rocio Flores, Barrangan Style

Situated just five miles from the hustle and bustle of the tourist center of Cancun is the five mile long island Isla Mujeres. Steep coasts, deep green vegetation and wide sandy beaches are surrounded by clear waters. Although this is no longer an insider tip, the island has lost none of its appeal. A heaven of tranquility awaits visitors to the Casa de los Sueños Resort and Spa, which is why you won't find any telephones and televisions in the eight rooms and the spacious villa. Sun, Moon, Harmony, Peace and Joy are not just room names, but are also representative of the design. Upon entering Joy, you immediately sense the cheerful atmosphere thanks to the bright colors. Balancing beige nuances await guests in the Harmony room. The Peace room with its Japanese elements is inspired by meditation. Architectonic elements typical of the country are masterfully combined with items from different countries and eras, which explains the Egyptian cotton bed sheets and sofas, which are sunk into the floor in the center of the room, reminiscent of 70's penthouse apartments.

Nur acht Kilometer vor dem umtriebigen Touristenzentrum Cancún liegt die nur acht Kilometer lange Isla Mujeres. Steilküsten, tiefgrüne Vegetation und breite Sandstrände sind von klarem Wasser umgeben. Obwohl längst kein Geheimtipp mehr, hat das Eiland wenig von seinen Reizen verloren. Wer in die Casa de los Sueños Resort and Spa kommt, findet hier einen Ort der Ruhe. Telefon und Fernseher gibt es in den acht Zimmern und der geräumigen Villa daher nicht. Sun, Moon, Harmony, Peace und Joy sind nicht nur Zimmernamen, sondern stehen stellvertretend für das Design. Wer Joy betritt, spürt dank leuchtender Farben sofort die heitere Atmosphäre. Ausgleichend wirkende Beige-Nuancen findet der Gast im Raum Harmony. Das Zimmer Peace erinnert mit japanischen Elementen an Meditation. Landestypische architektonische Elemente werden gekonnt mit Teilen aus verschiedenen Ländern und Epochen kombiniert. So besteht die Bettwäsche aus ägyptischer Baumwolle und Sofas, die in der Mitte des Raumes in den Boden eingelassen sind, erinnern an 70er-Jahre Penthouse-Wohnungen.

01 | It's just 20 minutes by boat to the peaceful resort from the hectic metropolis of Cancún.

Nur 20 Minuten sind es mit dem Boot von der hektischen Metropole Cancún in das ruhige Resort.

02 | Although the house only has eight rooms, the open lobbies are particularly spacious.

Obwohl das Haus nur acht Zimmer hat, sind die offenen Aufenthaltsbereiche besonders großzügig gestaltet.

03 | When darkness falls, lanterns guide the way.

Wenn die Sonne untergegangen ist, weisen Windlichter den Weg.

04 | On request the spa staff can combine different massage elements.

Auf Wunsch kombiniert das Personal im Spa verschiedene Massageelemente.

05 | Tales of swimming with dolphins during the day are told at the bar once the sun has set.

Wer tagsüber mit Delfinen geschwommen ist, kann abends davon an der Bar berichten.

01 | "Style is a privilege", is the saying at this hotel. This can also be said of the view from the terrace.

„Stil ist ein Privileg", heißt es im Hotel. Der Blick von der Terrasse ist es ebenfalls.

marina all suites | rio de janeiro . brazil

DESIGN: Joy Garrido, Pedro Paranaguá, Julinha Serrado, André Piva, Jairo de Sender, Beth Lucena, Tarcila Paiva, Luiz Fernando Grabowsky, Caco Borges, Paola Ribeiro, Beatrice Goldfeld

"Every guest is unique", according to the philosophy of this Brazilian house. Individuality is not only at the fore when it comes to the service of guests, but also in terms of design. And so the hotel merges the concept of boutique with design. Eight of the 38 spacious suites were designed by renowned Brazilian architects. Jairo de Sender concentrated on luxury wooden furniture with a masculine touch in his Onix-Suite. Beth Lucena focused on a cheerful atmosphere in the design of her Opala-Suite, in which white contrasts with vibrant tones. And design is also at the forefront in the standard suites, which are between 420 and 590 square feet. Lots of wood and warm earth tones give the rooms a cozy touch so every guest feels at home right away. However upon seeing the breathtaking ocean view from the large windows, it soon becomes clear that one is in an extra special place here. The house is situated in the Leblon part of town, right on the wide, fine-sandy beach. This is why it's not only the perfect starting point for endless strolls, but also for dancing the night away in the numerous bars of the area. Yet Leblon is not just a place for revelers. The residents also value the neighborhood because of its family-friendly and relaxed atmosphere.

„Jeder Gast ist einzigartig", lautet die Philosophie des brasilianischen Hauses. Individualität steht nicht nur bei der Betreuung der Gäste, sondern auch in punkto Design im Vordergrund. So verbindet das Hotel ein Boutique- mit einem Designkonzept. Acht der 38 geräumigen Suiten wurden von bekannten brasilianischen Architekten gestaltet. Jairo de Sender konzentrierte sich bei seiner Onix-Suite auf luxuriöses Holzmobiliar mit maskulinem Touch. Beth Lucena setzte bei der Gestaltung ihrer Opala-Suite auf eine fröhliche Atmosphäre, in der Weiß mit leuchtenden Tönen kontrastiert. Doch auch in den Standard-Suiten, die zwischen 39 und 55 Quadratmeter groß sind, kommt das Design nicht zu kurz. Viel Holz und warme Erdtöne lassen die Räume gemütlich wirken. So fühlt sich jeder Gast sofort wie zu Hause. Allerdings erinnert spätestens der atemberaubende Ozeanblick aus den großen Fenstern daran, dass man sich hier an einem ganz besonderen Ort befindet. Das Haus liegt im Stadtteil Leblon, direkt am breiten, feinsandigen Strand. Somit ist es der perfekte Ausgangspunkt für endlose Spaziergänge, aber auch für durchtanzte Nächte in den zahlreichen Bars des Viertels. Dabei ist Leblon nicht nur ein Ort für Nachtschwärmer. Die Anwohner schätzen den Stadtteil auch wegen seiner Familienfreundlichkeit und entspannten Atmosphäre.

02

02 | The central significance of the ocean for the residents of Rio de Janeiro can also be seen in the design of the Marina All Suites.

Welch zentrale Bedeutung der Ozean für die Bewohner Rio de Janeiros hat, lässt sich auch im Design des Marina All Suites ablesen.

03 | Closed doors are seldom here. Also the lounge is designed to be open and inviting.

Verschlossene Türen sind selten. Auch die Lounge ist offen und einladend gestaltet.

04 | André Piva designed the Ambar Suite. With its cherry-wood furniture and ethnic sculptures it is one of the most popular in the house.

André Piva konzipierte die Ambar-Suite. Mit ihrem Kirschholzmobiliar und den ethnischen Skulpturen gehört sie zu den beliebtesten des Hauses.

05 | If you're still not relaxed enough after a night in a king-size bed, a massage at the in-house spa will do the trick.

Wer nach einer Nacht im Kingsize-Bett noch nicht entspannt genug ist, kann sich im hauseigenen Spa massieren lassen.

hotel index

Country / Location	Address	Information	Architecture & Design	Page
Italy — Amalfi	Casa Angelina Via G. Capriglione 147 84010 Praiano (Sa) Amalfi Coast, Italy www.steinhotels.com/casaangelina	opened 2005 41 rooms, restaurant, bar, spa, indoor and outdoor pool. 90 minutes drive from the airport.	Marco de Luca, Francesco Savarese and Fusco Gennaro	8
France — Corsica	Casa del Mar Route de Palombaggia BP 93 20538 Porto-Vecchio Cedex South Corsica, France www.casadelmar.fr	opened 2004 2 suites, 2 junior suites, 4 superior junior suites, 4 deluxe double rooms, 4 superior double rooms, restaurant, lounge, bar, private beach, pool, spa, massage, hamam. 25 km from Figari Sud Corse Airport	Jean Francois Bodin Carole Marcellesi	14
Spain — Ibiza	Ses Pitreras c/Valladolid, 1-3 07839 S.Agustí des Vedrà Ibiza, Spain www.sespitreras.com	opened 2004 5 rooms and 2 suites, bar, restaurant, swimming pool. Nearest beach 200 meters, nearby Cala Bassa, Cala Comte, Cala Tarida. 15 km from Ibiza Town, 5 km from Sant Antoni and 10 km from airport.	Joan Lao	18
Spain — Marbella	The Beach House Urbanización El Chaparral, 340 km 203 29648 Mijas Costa, Spain www.beachhouse.nu	opened 2001 10 rooms, pool, lounge and bar, breakfast. 15-20 minutes by car from Málaga airport.	Kjell Sporrong	22
Portugal — Cascais	Farol Design Hotel Av. Rei Humberto II de Itália 7 2750-461 Cascais Portugal www.cascais.org	opened 2002 34 rooms and suites, restaurant, sushi lounge, bars. Outside pool bar, outdoor salt water swimming pool, sunbed terrace, ocean deck. 30 km from Lisbon airport	Cristina Santos Silva & Ana Meneses Cardoso, Carlos Miguel Dias (CM DIAS Arquitectos), Angela Basto & Paula Castro, Ana Salazar, José António Tenente, António Augustus, João Rôlo, Fátima Lopes, Miguel Vieira, Paulo Matos, Manuel Alves & José Manuel Gonçalves, Paulina Figueiredo, Arkadius	26

hotel index

Country/Location	Address	Information	Architecture & Design	Page
Greece — Santorini	Ikies Traditional Houses 847 02 Oia, Santorini Greece www.ikies.com	reopened 2000 3 studios, 3 maisonettes, 4 suites, 1 villa, 1 main pool. 7 out of 11 rooms with private hot tub on terrace, 3 rooms with steam room and hamam. Located in the village of Oia at the northern part of the island. 25 minutes (15 km) from the airport.	Akis Charalambous	30
Greece — Crete	Blue Palace Resort & Spa 72053 Elounda Greece www.starwoodhotels.com	opened 2003 252 rooms, restaurants, bars. Elounda Spa and thalassotherapy, massages, gym, saunas, hamams, jaccuzzis and 1 indoor heated pool, 2 outdoor pools with sea water, 1 outdoor fresh water pool. Located on the northeast coast of Crete at the Gulf of Elounda, just opposite the island of Spinalonga. 1 hour (78 km) from the airport.	Team around Angelos Angelopoulos 3SK Stylianides Costantza Sbokou	34
Turkey — Antalya	Hillside Su Konyaalti 07050 Antalya Turkey www.hillsidesu.com.	opened 2003 294 rooms, including 41 suites. Ball room, 8 meeting rooms, buffet and á la carte restaurants, lounge, bars, heated indoor and outdoor pools, spa. 15 km from the center of Antalya. 15 minutes drive from airport.	Eren Talu Yael Bahior Asli Eke Merve Yoneyman	38
UAE — Dubai	Madinat Jumeirah, the Arabian Resort PO Box 75157, Dubai UAE www.madinatjumeirah.com	opened 2004 867 rooms and suites 29 traditional courtyard summer houses. 45 restaurants and bars. Healthclub, Madinat Arena, theater, amphitheater, conference hall. 25 minutes from Dubai International Airport	KCA International Khuan Chew Design Principal Mirage Mille	42
Oman — Muscat	The Chedi Muscat P.O. Box 964, Al Khuwair Muscat Sultanate of Oman www.ghmhotels.com	opened 2003 151 rooms. Restaurant, pools, gym, spa. 20 minutes north of Muscat harbour. 12 km from Seeb International Airport in Al Ghubra.	Yaya Ibrahim Jean-Michel Gathy	46

hotel index | 161

hotel index

Country/Location	Address	Information	Architecture & Design	Page
Mauritius — Poste de Flacq	Constance Belle Mare Plage Poste de Flacq Mauritius www.bellemareplagehotel.com	reopened 2002 92 rooms, 137 junior suites, 6 luxury suites, 20 villas, 1 presidential villa, restaurants, bars, wellness center, two 18-hole golf courses. 60 minutes from airport.	Jean-Marc Eynaud Martin Branner Colin Okashimo	52
Mauritius — Wolmar	Taj Exotica Resort & Spa Wolmar, Flic en Flac Mauritius www.tajhotels.com	opened 2004 65 villas, 2 presidential suites, restaurants, lounge bar, yoga pavillion, taj spa, health club, activities, sightseeing, shopping, 45 minutes from airport.	Maurice Giraud Architects David Edwards/James Park Associates	56
Seychelles — North Island	North Island P.O. Box 1176, Victoria Mahe North Island Seychelles www.north-island.com	opened 2003, spa 2004 11 villas with lounge, plunge pool. Each villa is equipped with an electro-buggy and 2 bicycles. Cuisine—each menu is created individually. Sunset beach bar. Spa with outdoor area. PADI dive center, gym. 4 beaches including a private honeymoon beach. 15 minutes from Mahé by helicopter.	LIFE, Silvio Rech & Lesley Carstens	60
Kenya — Diani Beach	Alfajiri Villas P.O. Box 454 Diani Beach Kenya www.alfajirivillas.com	Cliff Villa opened 2000, Garden and Beach Villa opened 2004 12 rooms in 3 villas, massage and reflexology, dining area and private pool, sea view Gazzebos, located on the south coast in Diani, 1 hour from Mombasa Airport.	Marika Molinaro	64
Mozambique — Quirimbas Archipel	Matemo Island Resort Quirimbas Archipelago Cabo Delgado Province Mozambique www.matemoresort.com	opened 2004 24 chalets, restaurant, bar lounge, swimming pool, various water sports avtivities with diving and fishing center. 30 minutes flight transfer with a light aircraft from Pemba International Airport.	RSL Nikki McCarthy Interiors	68

hotel index

Country / Location		Address	Information	Architecture & Design	Page
South Africa	Hermanus	Birkenhead House 7th Avenue Voelklip, Hermanus, 7200 South Africa www.birkenheadhouse.com	opened 2003 11 suites most of them with sea views. Dining room, 3 pools one of them on dual levels. Spa, gym and treatment room. The whole hotel can be reserved for a maximum of 22 persons. Situated in Hermanus, 90 minutes from Cape Town.	Liz Biden and Ralph Krall Phil Biden and Michael Dall	72
Sri Lanka	Tangalle	Amanwella Bodhi Mawatha, Wella Wathuara, Godellawela Sri Lanka www.amanwella.com	opened 2005 30 rooms, restaurant, lounge bar, pool terrace, beach club, swimming pool, library, spa. 5 hours from Colombo International Airport.	Kerry Hill	78
Sri Lanka	Bentota	Saman Villas Aturuwela, Bentota Sri Lanka www.samanvilla.com	opened 1996 26 suites and 1 villa, restaurants, bar, pool, spa, tennis. Library, snooker, badminton, table tennis, and an All-Suite Luxury Garden Spa. Located on the south west coast of Sri Lanka, 92 km from the airport.	Geevaka de Soyza Murad Ismail	82
Maldives	North Male Atoll	Baros Maldives 39, Orchid Magu P.O. Box 2015 Male 20-02 Republic of Maldives www.baros.com	opened 2005. 75 villas, 3 restaurants, 2 bars. Spa, fitness centre, water sports, diving centre. Located on its own private island in the North Male Atoll. A 15 minute speedboat ride from Male International Airport.	Mohamed Shafeeg Anita Indra Dewi	86
Maldives	South Male Atoll	Anantara Resort Maldives P.O. Box 2014 Malé Dhigufinolhu South Male Atoll Republic of Maldives www.anantara.com	opened 2006 68 beachfront villas, 2 beachfront pool villas, 38 over-water suites and 2 over-water pool suites. Restaurant, bar, pool, spa, tennis, Terrazzo. 35 minutes from Male International Airport.	John Lightbody, Abacus Mohamed Shafeeg	90

hotel index

Country / Location	Address	Information	Architecture & Design	Page
Thailand — Phuket	Aleenta Resort and Spa Phuket - Phangnga Khao Pilai Beach Phangnga, Thailand www.aleenta.com/phuket	opened 2006 4 beachfront pool suites with plunge pools, 3 pool villas with luxury living room and pools, 8 ocean view lofts, 10 ocean view residences with 2 bedrooms, living, dining, kitchen and pools, 5 beachfront villas with 3 bedrooms, living, dining, kitchen and infinity pool. Restaurant, bar, spa and pool lounge. 20 minutes from Phuket International Airport.	Simple Space Design Shawwah Home Décor	94
Thailand — Krabi	Costa Lanta 212 Moo 1, Saladan Amphur Koh Lanta Krabi, Thailand www.costalanta.com	opened 2002 22 bungalows with private terrace beachfront bar and restaurant, traditional thai and relax massages. Location on Klong Dao Beach, a beach cove in the northern part of Lanta Yai Island. 10 min from Saladan town and public pier and ferries from Krabi town and Phi Phi islands. 80 km from Krabi Airport, 190 km from Phuket Airport.	Duangrit Bunnag	100
Thailand — Koh Samui	Sala Samui Resort and Spa 10/9 Moo 5, Baan Plai Lam Bophut Koh Samui Suratthani 84320 Thailand www.salasamui.com	opened 2004 69 villas and suites. 2 restaurants, bar, wine cellar, swimming pool, spa, massage, sea-, city- and moutain-tours. Located at North Choeng Mon Beach, 3 km from the airport.	Be Gray	104
Austalia Tropical North Queensland	Voyages Dunk Island Tropical North Queensland Australia www.dunk-island.com	opened 1934, reopened 2004 160 rooms. Restaurants, bars and lounge. Spa, sports, golf course. No airport or aerodrome on the island.	Justin Long	108
Australia — Surfers Paradise	Couran Cove Island Resort PO Box 224 Runaway Bay Australia www.couran-cove.com.au	opened 1998 313 rooms, 4 restaurants. The resort offers over 100 different activities. Located on South Stradbroke Island. 40 minutes by ferry from the Hope Harbour terminal. 55 minutes from Brisbane Airport and 45 minutes from Coolangatta Airport (Gold Coast).	Daryl Jackson	112

hotel index

Country / Location	Address	Information	Architecture & Design	Page
New Zealand — Bay of Islands	Eagles Nest Kohanga Ekara 60 Tapeka Road Bay of Islands New Zealand www.eaglesnest.co.nz	opened 2000 4 villas with private lap pools, spa with sunset decks. Located on a secluded 75 acre private estate with views over the Bay of Islands, a 40 minute flight from Auckland to Kerikeri the closest airport.	Sandra and Daniel Biskind	116
French Polynesia — Bora Bora	Bora Bora Nui Resort and Spa Motu Toopua, Nunue Bora Bora French Polynesia www.boraboranui.com	opened 2002 120 villas and suites, deck glass floor panels in over water villas, 2 restaurants, 2 bars, swimming pool, sauna, hammam, beauty salon, fitness center. Located on Motu Toopua 15 min boat ride from the airport and 10 min boat ride from the main village.	Pierre Lacombe Lulu Wane	120
Florida — Miami South Beach	The Setai 2001 Collins Avenue Miami Beach, FL 33139 USA www.setai.com	opened 2005 125 suites with one, two, and three bedrooms, 929 m² penthouse with rooftop pool. Restaurant, lounge bar and beach bar. Three beachfront pools. Spa with ocean view. Fitness center, yoga, tai chi. Water sports, golf, tennis. Located on the beach of South Beach. 20 minutes from the airport.	Jaya Pratomo Ibrahim from Jaya & Associates Jean Michel Gathy from Denniston International	124
British West Indies — Barbuda	The Beach House Barbuda Barbuda British West Indies www.thebeachhouse-barbuda.com	opened 2004 20 suites, restaurant (Club House, Chef Andrea Coppola). Spa services available anywhere on property. 30 minutes from VC Bird International Airport.	OBM International Linda Blair & Associates	128
Caribbean — St. Barthélemy	Eden Rock St. Barthélemy Caribbean www.edenrockhotel.com	opened 1995 33 suites some with private pools. Restaurant, bar. About 1.5 km from the airport.	Jane Matthews David Matthews	132

hotel index

Country / Location	Address	Information	Architecture & Design	Page
Mexico — Puerto Vallarta	Las Alamandas Km 83 Carretera Barra de Navidad, Puerto Vallarta Quémaro, Jalisco 48980 Mexico www.alamandas.com	opened 1990 6 villas with 15 suites for maximum 30 guests, villas with indoor and outdoor lounge areas, high-pitched tile roofs, private terraces. Palapa beach club, restaurant and bar. Conference room. Fitness center, tennis court, horseback riding swimming pool, golf course nearby. 2 hours drive from Manzanillo Airport.	Gabriel Nunez Isabel Goldsmith	138
Mexico — Veracruz	Hotel Azúcar Km 83,5 Carretera Federal Nautla – Poza Rica c.p. 93588 Monte Gordo Veracruz, Mexico http://www.hotelazucar.com	opened 2005 20 bungalows. Restaurant, lounge, pool, library. 30 minutes from the north of the village of San Rafael. 1,5 hour drive from the airport of Poza Rica.	Carlos Couturier Elias Adam and Jose Robredo	142
Mexico — Riviera Maya	Esencia Playa Xpu-Ha Riviera Maya Mexico www.hotelesencia.com	opened 2006 29 accommodations in different suites and cottages, terraces and plunge pools. Restaurant Sal y Fuego. Organic spa specialized in fito-therapy. Yoga, couples' spa suites, jacuzzis. 45 minutes from Cancun Airport.	Prohotel International Alfonso Nuñez	146
Mexico — Isla Mujeres	Casa de los Sueños Resort and Spa Carretera a Garrafón Fracc. Turqueza lote 9 A y B Isla Mujeres, Q. Roo, Mexico www.casadelossuenosresort.com	opened 2003 9 rooms and suites, 1 villa, 2 restaurants, lounge, sun deck. From Isla Mujeres to Cancun 1 hour and 30 minutes.	Alma Rocio Flores Barragan Style	152
Brazil — Rio de Janeiro	Marina All Suites Av. Delfim Moreira 696, Praia do Leblon Rio de Janeiro Brazil www.marinaallsuites.com.br	opened 1999 38 suites, beach view, restaurant, cinema, fitness center, swimming pool, massage, steam sauna. Cable TV, CD player, voice mail, internet access, roof top with glass walls. 25 km from Antonio Jobim International Airport.	Joy Garrido, Pedro Paranaguá, Julinha Serrado, Beth Lucena, Tarcila Paiva, André Piva	156

architects & designers

Name	Hotel	Page
3SK Stylianides	Blue Palace Resort & Spa	34
Elias Adam	Hotel Azúcar	142
Manuel Alves	Farol Design Hotel	26
Team around		
Angelos Angelopoulos	Blue Palace Resort & Spa	34
Arkadius	Farol Design Hotel	26
António Augustus	Farol Design Hotel	26
Yael Bahior	Hillside Su	38
Be Gray	Sala Samui Resort & Spa	104
Angela Basto	Farol Design Hotel	26
Liz Biden	Birkenhead House	72
Phil Biden	Birkenhead House	72
Sandra and Daniel Biskind	Eagles Nest Kohanga Ekara	116
Linda Blair & Associates	The Beach House Barbuda	128
Jean Francois Bodin	Casa del Mar	14
Caco Borges	Marina All Suites	156
Martin Branner	Constance Belle Mare Plage	52
Duangrit Bunnag	Costa Lanta	100
Ana Meneses Cardoso	Farol Design Hotel	26
Paula Castro	Farol Design Hotel	26
Akis Charalambous	Ikies Traditional Houses	30
Khuan Chew	Madinat Jumeirah, the Arabian Resort	42
Carlos Couturier	Hotel Azúcar	142
Michael Dall	Birkenhead House	72
David Edwards/James Park Associates	Taj Exotica Resort & Spa	56
Marco de Luca	Casa Angelina	8
Geevaka de Soyza	Saman Villas	82
Design Principal	Madinat Jumeirah, the Arabian Resort	42
Anita Indra Dewi	Baros Maldives	86
Carlos Miguel Dias (CM Dias Arquitectos)	Farol Design Hotel	26
Asli Eke	Hillside Su	38
Jean-Marc Eynaud	Constance Belle Mare Plage	52
Paulina Figueiredo	Farol Design Hotel	26
Joy Garrido	Marina All Suites	156
Jean-Michel Gathy	The Chedi Muscat	46
Jean Michel Gathy from Denniston International	The Setai	124
Fusco Gennaro	Casa Angelina	8
Maurice Giraud Architects	Taj Exotica Resort & Spa	56
Beatrice Goldfeld	Marina All Suites	156
Isabel Goldsmith	Las Alamandas	138
José Manuel Gonçalves	Farol Design Hotel	26
Kerry Hill	Amanwella	78
Yaya Ibrahim	The Chedi Muscat	46
Jaya Pratomo Ibrahim from Jaya & Associates	The Setai	124
Murad Ismail	Saman Villas	82
Daryl Jackson	Couran Cove Island Resort	112
KCA International	Madinat Jumeirah, the Arabian Resort	42
Ralph Krall	Birkenhead House	72
Pierre Lacombe	Bora Bora Nui Resort & Spa	120
Joan Lao	Ses Pitreras	18
LIFE	North Island	60
John Lightbody from Abacus	Anantara Maldives	90
Justin Long	Voyages Dunk Island	108
Fátima Lopes	Farol Design Hotel	26
Beth Lucena	Marina All Suites	156
Carole Marcellesi	Casa del Mar	14
Paulo Matos	Farol Design Hotel	26
David Matthews	Eden Rock	132
Jane Matthews	Eden Rock	132
Nikki McCarthy Interiors	Matemo Island Resort	68
Mirage Mille	Madinat Jumeirah, the Arabian Resort	42
Marika Molinaro	Alfajiri Villas	64
Gabriel Nunez	Las Alamandas	138
Alfonso Nuñez	Esencia	146
OBM International	The Beach House Barbuda	128
Colin Okashimo	Constance Belle Mare Plage	52
Pedro Paranaguá	Marina All Suites	156
Tarcila Paiva	Marina All Suites	156
André Piva	Marina All Suites	156
Prohotel International	Esencia	146
Paola Ribeiro	Marina All Suites	156
Jose Robredo	Hotel Azúcar	142
João Rôlo	Farol Design Hotel	26
RSL	Matemo Island Resort	68
Ana Salazar	Farol Design Hotel	26
Cristina Santos Silva	Farol Design Hotel	26
Francesco Savarese	Casa Angelina	8
Costantza Sbokou	Blue Palace Resort & Spa	34
Julinha Serrado	Marina All Suites	156
Jairo de Sender	Marina All Suites	156
Luiz Fernando Grabowsky	Marina All Suites	156
Mohamed Shafeeg	Baros Maldives	86
Mohamed Shafeeg	Anantara Resort Maldives	90
Shawwah Home Décor	Aleenta Resort and Spa Phuket – Phangnga	94
Silvio Rech & Lesley Carstens	North Island	60
Alma Rocio Flores	Casa de los Sueños Resort and Spa	152
Simple Space Design	Aleenta Resort and Spa Phuket – Phangnga	94
Kjell Sporrong	The Beach House	128
Eren Talu	Hillside Su	38
José António Tenente	Farol Design Hotel	26
Miguel Vieira	Farol Design Hotel	26
Lulu Wane	Bora Bora Nui Resort & Spa	120
Merve Yoneyman	Hillside Su	38

photo credits

Name	Hotel	Page (Photos)
courtesy The Chedi Muscat	The Chedi Muscat	Cover
Martin Nicholas Kunz	Constance Belle Mare Plage	Backcover
courtesy Aleenta	Aleenta Resort and Spa Phuket - Phangnga	7, 94 (all)
courtesy Alfajiri Villas	Alfajiri Villas	64 (all)
courtesy Amanresorts	Amanwella	79, 80
Roland Bauer	Madinat Jumeirah, the Arabian Resort	44
courtesy Blue Palace Resort & Spa	Blue Palace Resort & Spa	34 (all)
courtesy Bora Bora Nui Resort & Spa	Bora Bora Nui Resort & Spa	120 (all)
courtesy Casa Angelina	Casa Angelina	8 (all)
courtesy Casa de los Sueños Resort and Spa	Casa de los Sueños Resort and Spa	152 (all)
courtesy Casa del Mar	Casa del Mar	14 (all)
courtesy Costa Lanta	Costa Lanta	100 (all)
courtesy Couran Cove Island Resort	Couran Cove Island Resort	112 (all)
courtesy Eagles Nest Kohanga Ekara	Eagles Nest Kohanga Ekara	116 (all)
courtesy Eden Rock	Eden Rock	132 (all)
courtesy Farol Design Hotel	Farol Design Hotel	26 (all)
courtesy Hillside Su	Hillside Su	38 (all)
courtesy Hotel Azúcar	Hotel Azúcar	142 (all)
courtesy Ikies Traditional Houses	Ikies Traditional Houses	5, 30 (all)
Gavin Jackson	Amanwella	78, 81
	Anantara Resort Maldives	90 (all)
	Baros Maldives	5, 86 (all)
	Marina All Suites	156 (all)
	Saman Villas	4, 82 (all)
courtesy Matemo Island Resort	Matemo Island Resort	7, 68 (all)
courtesy Sala Samui Resort & Spa	Sala Samui Resort & Spa	104 (all)
courtesy Ses Pitreras	Ses Pitreras	18 (all)
courtesy The Beach House	The Beach House	22 (all)
courtesy The Beach House Barbuda	The Beach House Barbuda	128 (all)
courtesy The Chedi Muscat	The Chedi Muscat	46 (all)
courtesy The Setai	The Setai	124, 125
courtesy Voyages	Voyages Dunk Island	108 (all)

all other photos by Martin Nicholas Kunz

imprint

Bibliographic information published by Die Deutsche Bibliothek. Die Deutsche Bibliothek lists this publication in the Deutsche Nationalbibliografie; detailed bibliographic data are available on the internet at http://ddb.de
ISBN 10: 3-89986-078-0
ISBN 13: 978-3-89986-078-8

1st edition
© 2006 Martin Nicholas Kunz
© 2006 fusion publishing gmbh, stuttgart . los angeles
© 2006 avedition GmbH, Ludwigsburg
All rights reserved.

Printed in Austria
by Vorarlberger Verlagsanstalt AG, Dornbirn

Editors | Martin Nicholas Kunz, Patricia Massó
Editorial coordination | Rosina Geiger, Hanna Martin, Anne-Kathrin Meier
Copy editing | Gabriele Franz
Translations | C.E.T. Central European Translations

Layout | Jasmina Bremer
Imaging | Jan Hausberg; pixgreen-media factory, Stuttgart

avedition GmbH
Königsallee 57 | 71638 Ludwigsburg | Germany
p +49-7141-1477391 | f +49-7141-1477399
www.avedition.com | contact@avedition.com

Further information and links at
www.bestdesigned.com
www.fusion-publishing.com

Texts (pages) | Bärbel Holzberg (42), Corina Kayfel (22, 78, 86), Anna Streubert (52, 94, 124), riva-medien (8, 30, 68, 82, 90, 116, 128, 142), Carolin Schöngarth (14, 108, 112, 138, 146, 152, 156), Heinfried Tacke (100), Bettina Winterfeld (editorial, 18, 34, 64, 72, 104, 120, 132), all other texts by fusion publishing.

Special thanks to Kirsten Beck, Kleber PR Network | Sandra Beltran, Prohotel International | Clara Botero, The Setai | Annika Brandenburger, ArabellaSheraton Hotelmanagement GmbH | Alberto Buil, Ses Pitreras | Jorge Cosme, Farol Design Hotel | Miguel Cunat, Sri Lanka In Style | Ali Enginertan, Hillside Su | Basak Erson, Hillside Su | Alfredo Freyre, Marina All Suites | Gelmy Garrido, Casa de los Sueños Resort and Spa | Gianluca, Casa del Mar | Damien Hanger, Voyages | Mike Hiles, MPH PR | Himaj Jayasinghe, Saman Villas | Ingo Jacob, Travel Consultants Africa | Kasma Kantavanih, Costa Lanta | Anchalika Kijkanakorn, Aleenta | Supakorn Kijkanakorn, Aleenta | Charlotte von Koenen, Blue Palace Resort & Spa | Lore Koenig, The Chedi Muscat | Lorraine and Graham, Eagles Nest Kohanga Ekara | Marit-Andrea Meineke, ZFL PRCo | Rafael Micha, Grupo Habita | Fabrizio Molinaro, Alfajiri Villas | Ashley MontBlanc, Laura Davidson Public Relations | Nimalka Morahella, Sri Lanka In Style | Lee-Anne Nichols, Couran Cove Island Resort | Anjali Nihalchand, Amanresorts | Omapatt Nuntapanish, Sala Resorts and Spas | Eléonore Petin, Bora Bora Nui Resort & Spa | José A. C. Pascoal, Farol Design Hotel | Laura Pettitt, Brandman PR | Nopparat Pongwatanakulsiri, Anantara Resorts | Birgit Rapp, Text & Aktion | Christiane Reiter, Constance Belle Mare Plage | Frauke Rothschuh, Text & Aktion | Helen Schröger, Schaffelhuber Communications | Christos Seferiades, Ikies Traditional Houses | Laura Selman, The Stein Group | Bruce Simpson, North Island | Devyani Singh, The Setai | Kathy Wayland, Birkenhead House | Iréne Westerberg, The Beach House | Avon Wong, Amanresorts for their support.

Martin Nicholas Kunz
1957 born in Hollywood. Founder of fusion publishing creating content for architecture, design, travel, and lifestyle publications.

Patricia Massó
1962 born in Stuttgart. Working as marketing and PR consultant with an emphasis on hotel business and editor of several hotel and design books.

best designed:
ecological hotels
affordable hotels
modular houses
outdoor living
hotel pools

best designed hotels:
asia pacific
americas
europe I (urban)
europe II (countryside)

best designed wellness hotels:
asia pacific
americas
europe
africa & middle east

All books are released in German and English